Overcoming the Digital Divide

Overcoming the Digital Divide

How to use Social Media and Digital Tools to
reinvent yourself and your career

By Shelly Palmer
and Mike Raffensperger

YORK HOUSE PRESS

Library of Congress Control Number: 2011927346

ISBN: 978-0-9791956-7-9

York House Press
800 Westchester Avenue, Suite 641 North
Rye Brook, NY 10573

Dedication

In loving memory of my father, Lon T. Palmer, who was fond of saying, "Don't tell me about it, just do it."

—Shelly Palmer

To those who keep me grounded but always looking up: Beth, Mom and Dad.

—Mike Raffensperger

Contents

Acknowledgments

First and foremost, I would like to thank Mike Raffensperger, who truly co-authored this work. His tireless devotion to synthesizing, adapting and editing this book was nothing short of amazing. His contributions were invaluable and I cannot thank him enough.

I would also like to thank my good friend Richard Sellers for his comments, criticisms and suggestions. Among other things, Richard is the chairman of MENG, the Marketing Executives Networking Group. He is a marketer's marketer and one of my most powerful secret weapons.

Thanks to my wife, Debbie, whose honest, constructive criticism is much needed and always appreciated.

A very special thank you to Penny Holt, who made this book actually happen!

And, a quick shout out to Amanda Peters, Aanarav Sareen, Zach Superior, Mike McGregor and my brother, Jason Palmer, for all of their help. And a tip of the hat to editor Ellen Lohman and the book and cover designers at Concise.

About the Authors

Shelly Palmer is the host of NBC Universal's Live Digital with Shelly Palmer, a weekly half-hour television show about living and working in a digital world. He is Fox 5 New York's On-air Tech Expert (WNYW-TV) and the host of Fox Television's Shelly Palmer Digital Living. He also hosts United Stations Radio Network's MediaBytes, a daily syndicated radio report that features insightful commentary and a unique insider's take on the biggest stories in technology, media and entertainment. He is managing director of Advanced Media Ventures Group, LLC, an industry-leading advisory and business development firm, and the president of the National Academy of Television Arts & Sciences, NY, the organization that bestows the coveted Emmy® Awards.

He is the patented inventor of the underlying technology for Enhanced Television (Who Wants to Be a Millionaire, Monday Night Football), the most popular form of interactive television in the United States, and OCAP (OpenCable Application Platform), an operating system layer designed for consumer electronics that connect to a cable television system. He has been nominated twice for an Emmy® Award, and his professional vitae includes years of experience in television production and musical composition.

A prolific composer, Palmer received the American Society of Composers, Authors and Publishers' (ASCAP's) 12th Annual Film and Television Music Award for ABC's hit series Spin City. He was also recognized the following season in the category of "Most Performed Television Themes." Palmer's music credits include the theme songs for Live with Regis & Kelly, Rivera Live and MSNBC, as well as the digital debut of the "real" cat singing the classic "Meow, Meow, Meow, Meow." He is a weekly columnist for the Jack Myers Media Business Report and the Huffington Post and a technology commentator for CNN and CNNi.

Palmer is the author of Television Disrupted (York House Press, 2008), the seminal book about the technological, economic, and sociological forces that are changing everything.

Mike Raffensperger currently serves as the Vice President of Strategy and Creative Development for Magnet Media, a New York City-based digital production studio and marketing services firm. A passionate digital storyteller, Raffensperger has produced and overseen Webby Award-honored digital programming from viral shorts to broadcast–quality serials for an audience of millions. As a champion of social and new media marketing, he has designed and directed online campaigns for dozens of top-tier media and technology companies, including Apple, Microsoft, Adobe, Google, the Sundance Film Festival, ABC, NBC, Showtime and Paramount Pictures.

Mr. Raffensperger has written and spoken extensively on topics of branded entertainment, online marketing and viral digital programming. He regularly serves as a guest lecturer at New York University's Institute in Entertainment and Events Marketing and as a mentor at the Bay Area Video Coalition Producer's Institute, a MacArthur Foundation-funded residency program for independent producers and public broadcasters. His work has appeared on 1he Huffington Post, MSNBC.com, ReadWriteWeb, CMO.com, ProBlogger and Zoom In Online.

He is the co-author of Digital Media for Business, a Top 10 Kindle bestseller offering a primer on the doing of business in the digital age. He is a current Fellow with the Punch Sulzberger Media Executive Residency Program at Columbia University's School of Journalism and holds an undergraduate degree in Business Administration from Messiah College.

About the Book

A Note about Terms of Art and Technical Descriptions

Throughout this book, you will see words that look like English but are actually terms of art (technical terms) that have very specific professional definitions. Wherever possible, I try to define these terms contextually, in endnotes or in the Glossary. I think it is important for you to know at least some of these terms and acronyms by heart.

When I think it is really important for you to memorize a technical term, it will be defined in a "Digital Dictionary" box. Don't overuse these terms; just use them correctly, and you will be well on your way to obtaining your Digital Citizenship.

It is important to realize that there are very few technological absolutes. So, in my quest to simplify the technological descriptions herein, I am going to leave out lots of stuff that would not be helpful in understanding the bigger picture. I apologize in advance to the rather large constituency of hard-core techno-geeks who will consider this an unforgivable sin.

DIGITAL DICTIONARY

Digital Native:

Refers to anyone who grew up with 21st- century technology (i.e., anyone born after 1980). Digital natives share a common global culture that is defined by certain attributes and experiences related to how they interact with information technologies, information itself, other people and institutions.

Digital Immigrant:

Refers to anyone who grew up without 21st- century technology (i.e., anyone born before 1970) but has adapted to and adopted its use to some extent. Digital immigrants often pick up the traits and characteristics of digital natives, such as a trial-and-error approach to technology and an appreciation of information filtering and processing over information retention.

Who Should Read This Book?

Who should read this book? Those who know they need to know more about this new digital world to survive and prosper and think of it as a great journey.

If you are overwhelmed by technology and the modern world's pace of change, this is the book for you. In these pages you will find simple answers to the most pressing questions about how to live, work and prosper in an ever-increasingly digital world.

Who Should Not Read This Book?

If you are a self-described "Tech Guru," this book is not for you. If you just don't care about what everyone is talking about because "you don't have time for computers and smartphones," there is nothing here for you.

If you are happy that you do not know what's happening in the world around you, put this book down now.

Introduction

The original title of this book was, "49 & F*#ked! How to reinvent yourself and your career for the 21st- century economy." As you can imagine, it was not a publisher-friendly title. And, to be fair, it was not a particularly uplifting proposition. How many of us really want to admit that we have wasted the better part of our careers? We haven't, of course. But when you're competing with people who are fluent geekspeakers and self-described technocrats, presentations and job interviews can be very depressing, which is why I thought the name worked.

However, after some counsel from Richard Sellers, my personal marketing guru, I renamed the book, "Overcoming the Digital Divide." It is a much more SEO/SEM-friendly, brand, and publisher-safe title. And it offers an uplifting message: You can overcome the digital divide!

Do you need to? Only if you want to prosper in the 21st- century. Can you? Yes you can. No matter how technophobic you think you are. You can do this.

iPhone or Android? Do you have an opinion? Mac or PC? Are you the one to ask? IE, Firefox or Chrome? Can you give guidance? If not, you are not alone. To most people, this is geekspeak and, here's a little secret, most people who say they have the answers really don't. The good news ... after reading this book, you will!

So get ready. We're going on a short journey. I'll see you on the other side of the digital divide.

Chapter 1: Overcoming the Digital Divide

That Which Does Not Kill Us Makes Us Stronger

This is my favorite way to paraphrase Friedrich Nietzsche's famous quote *"Was ihn nicht umbringt, macht ihn starker"* (What does not kill him, makes him stronger). It doesn't matter how you like to say it, it's a remarkable perspective on the value of your experience. You may be a little "long in the tooth" or just an old soul, but the fact that you are still here says something extraordinary about you. You survived, you're relatively healthy, you're of sound mind (more or less) and you're thinking about your future. These are very good things.

We're going to use every bit of your experience to plan your future. Every boss who tortured you, every co-worker who screwed you, every vendor who let you down, everything bad that has ever happened in your career has made you stronger. Believe it ... it is the truth.

Of course, the good experiences are as big a part of who you are as the bad. But it is the bad experiences, the mistakes and the battles (both won and lost), that you will use to your advantage now.

Your previous experiences will allow you to make "new" mistakes instead of "old" ones. Grown-ups who have attained a "certain age" have the luxury of having made a zillion errors of varying sizes and complexities over the course of their careers. The new kid, 20 years your junior (who is looking for your job), has not had the pleasure of screwing up big time and living to tell about it.

You Don't Need to Be the Fittest, Just the Most Adaptable

"Survival of the fittest" is a misinterpretation of the thesis of Charles Darwin's 1859 classic, "On the Origin of Species by Means of Natural Selection." It is much better described as "survival of the most adaptable." All things being equal, being the fittest may make you more likely to pass on your genes to future generations (which is what natural selection is all about). But being the most adaptable makes you more likely to survive extraordinary circumstances that might otherwise kill you (thereby preventing you from passing on your genes at all). The very definition of a survivor is someone who had the ability to adapt to unanticipated (sometimes catastrophic) change and lived to tell the tale.

How many of us have reacted to outside stimuli and lived to tell about it? Of course, this rhetorical question applies to the lessons from our buddy Nietzsche as well. But, in this case, I'm talking about decisions (good or bad) that you may have made during your career that, in hindsight, changed the course of your life. If you go back and make a list of them – there shouldn't be more than a handful – you will be amazed at how random they seem on paper. Following a significant other someplace, meeting someone at a bar, seeing an ad in the paper, hearing about an opportunity from a friend – the list is virtually endless. Random, but endless.

How remarkable is it that anyone thinks they can control their destiny? I'm not talking about divine intervention; I'm simply stating the obvious: small random decisions are responsible for an inordinately large proportion of how our personal futures unfold.

I bring this up because I want you to understand that reinventing yourself and your career is a conscious decision that will require a serious commitment. We are going to use what you already know, to be sure. But we are also going to spend time accumulating new knowledge and new techniques. More importantly, we are going to learn how to analyze problems with the specific intention of using your newly acquired skills to solve them.

This actually needs a little more clarification. I could teach an average 11th grader enough calculus to solve a calculus problem. Math teachers do this in high schools all over the world every day. On the other hand, you would need a very different kind of mathematical training to observe the real world, see a problem and understand that calculus is the appropriate mathematical tool to solve it. This is not a subtle point. You could memorize the pages in this book, and the tools, tips and techniques might be of some help. However, if you bring your experience to these pages and approach the digital world as if it were no different than the world you experience every day, you will come away with basic skills you need to recognize problems that can be solved with digital tools. And with a little practice, you will understand how to break those problems down into action items that you can cover or feel comfortable managing.

What We Can Learn from Yoda

I love Yoda. He is by far my favorite sage. While I must admit I was a little bummed when he couldn't kick the Emperor's butt in Episode III, that doesn't take away from his formidable Jedi wisdom. "Try not. Do ... or do not. There is no try," says the Jedi Master to Luke Skywalker. Luke babbles some candy-ass excuse about his spacecraft being too big, and Yoda admonishes, "That is why you fail."

The only problem with pop-culture psychobabble is that it makes people believe that there are simple, wizened phrases that, if adhered to, will change your life. This assumption is patently wrong!

"Believe in yourself." "There is no 'I' in Team." "When one door closes, another door opens." Who writes this stuff? Pop-culture psychobabble (like you find in self-help books) really can't change your life. Only you can do that. (Wow, even that sounds like pop-culture psychobabble.)

Reinventing yourself is very hard work. It requires you to spend a great deal of time out of your comfort zone. Just to complete our cliché paragraph: If it were easy, everyone would do it. So, make Yoda proud and fully commit to overcoming the digital divide. It will be a giant step toward translating the value of your accumulated intellectual property into wealth.

The Unique Qualities of the Challenge

Interestingly, there is no established dogma or degree in the doing of digital work and life. A woman called me up after attending one of my seminars and said, "I didn't learn one thing I could not have learned on my own." I laughed, and she asked me what I was laughing about. And I told her that I didn't teach her one thing that I didn't learn on my own. The difference is that it took me years to amass the knowledge, filter it and learn to communicate it in usable chunks. I asked her if she had that kind of time to invest in her digital education. She laughed and said that she hadn't thought about it that way.

Of course you can learn everything I'm going to cover in these pages on your own. That's how the digital natives learned it. They learned by trial and error, watching their friends, experimenting, making mistakes, accidentally wiping their hard drives, losing data, downloading viruses, trusting utility programs that crashed their systems and on and on and on.

But you probably don't have that kind of time on your hands. So, this book is for you!

The Digital Divide Is a Socio-Techno Divide

The socio-techno divide is an upward-moving blurry line that defines the boundary between people who "get" digital by osmosis and those who have to deal with the reality that about a third of the current work force doesn't have a personal reference for the terms "dial the phone" or "sounds like a broken record."

Are you a member of the TV generation or part of the digital revolution? It's pretty easy to tell. The "space age" ended circa 1980 as the "information age" began. If you were born before 1980, you are part of the TV generation; if you are younger than that, you are either a digital immigrant or a digital native.

Now, of course there are many variations on this theme. At this writing, I put the practical socio-techno divide between 37 and 40 years old. My reasoning and supporting research are purely "armchair." If your idea of kicking back after a long day at school was hitting the sofa with a box of Cracker Jacks and a glass of Tang (because that's what the astronauts drank), you're a member of the TV generation. If your idea of recreation using a video screen includes coming home and playing a quad-split, first-person shooter on Xbox 360 with friends from around the world, drinking a Red Bull (with or without vodka) while munching on chocolate-covered coffee beans and Doritos (Nacho cheese flavor, so you cover two food groups), you're probably not a member of the TV generation.

If you don't know what a "quad-split, first-person shooter" is, you're on the high side of the socio-techno divide. If you don't care what a "quad-split, first-person shooter" is, you are missing the point of this book. Your

DIGITAL DICTIONARY

Quad-split, first-person shooter:

"Quad-split" means splitting a video screen into four quadrants. "First-person shooter" is the generic term for bang-em-up, shoot-em-up video games where gameplay is predominantly from the protagonist's point of view.

age doesn't matter, but you must be willing to learn about new forms of technology, media and entertainment that are on the other side of the digital divide. I am a card-carrying member of the TV generation, and proud of it. I have also been immersed in digital technology since before the personal computer was invented and have spent the better part of three decades using the efficiency of digital tools to enhance my career, make more money and create more of the one thing we all have too little of and value the most – personal time.

To overcome the digital divide, you must forget about the socio-techno divide. Yes, digital natives think and act differently than you do. Yes, they have a natural understanding of "how" to do certain things that you either had to learn or still have to learn. But when you're done reading this book, you will know enough about the digital tools you need to master to become a serious competitor.

Conventions of Computing

There are conventions of computing, just as there are conventions of theater or any other creative endeavor. You know many of them already. When you have a computer program open, there's a bar at the top of your screen. Mac or PC, it doesn't matter. There's a bar. You see it so often, you don't even think about it. You know that if you put your cursor over the word "File," you are going to see a bunch of options having to do with opening, closing, importing and exporting files. It doesn't matter what program you are running. This is a convention of computing. There are other words you see in the bar all of the time, such as "Edit," "View," "Window" and "Help," and each program has some special words,

---

Can you instantly tell whether a screen shot of a computer program is Mac or PC? It's easy. Almost every Mac OS X window has three little circles on the top left. They glow red, yellow and green from left to right. PC programs running under the Microsoft Windows operating system have a small white X in a red box on the right side of their program windows. It's that simple.

Don't confuse your operating systems. OS X runs only on machines made by Apple (with a few exceptions). As popular as Mac hardware is, it accounts for only 8% of the computers in the world. For all practical purposes, Microsoft Windows is running on everything else.

Want a quick way to prove you are irrelevant in the information age? Pull a screen shot of a Mac-only program and tell your boss you want to deploy it in your office (which is filled with PCs running Microsoft Windows) — that will go a long way toward getting you downsized.

---

such as "Format" or "Insert," depending on what the programs are supposed to do for you.

You know that when you put your cursor over these words, they become the focus of the program and they are highlighted. You know quite a bit about how these primary features operate. In fact, when you get a new program and an updated version of a program you know well, you will often browse through the menu bar looking for new or changed features.

It is this sense of exploration, trial and error, just goofing around that separates kids from grown-ups in the digital world. Digital natives have a well-defined set of expectations regarding the "doing of computing"; other people, not so much.

49 and F@#ked

On the last day of his corporate life, Murray, a 49-year-old middle manager for a large pharmaceutical company, entered the conference room as excited as he had ever been. He was an online monster now – he knew how to use the Internet, he could search Google as well as anyone, he had aggregated a list of key insights – in fact, he had some websites to talk about. This was going to be his meeting, his day. He was going to show everyone.

There were a few of the new young kids in the room, and of course Murray's boss was there, having just finished the previous meeting. Murray's entrance caused a break in the small talk – and then it happened. "Hey, Murray," yelled Spike, a 23-year-old head-banger who had obviously not had a very good experience with the business end of a tattoo needle, "what's the URL of that site you were so excited about?" Ready to kick some tattooed, body-pierced butt, Murray began to speak, "H T T P colon slash slash w w w ..." The room went silent as Spike quietly said, "Got that, man. Just give me the URL."

At that moment, Murray was toast! Poor Murray. He had no idea that by speaking each of the letters in the URL, he was not telling anyone in the room what he knew; he was telling them what he didn't know. Murray didn't last long. Two months later, after countless other tech faux pas, he was fired – the latest victim of downsizing. This does not have to happen to you!

The sad news is that Murray didn't even know what he did wrong. And he will probably never find out. As in so many other situations, it's not what you say, but how you say it.

Almost every website address starts with "http://" (upper or lower case – it doesn't matter). It stands for hyper-text transfer protocol, and it tells your web browser to expect to receive data in that format. And every site on the World Wide Web begins with "www." It stands for World Wide Web. When you are telling someone about a URL (uniform resource locator), all you have to say is the name and its extension, for example, google.com or ap.org – nothing more. There is another commonly used prefix, "https://," which stands for hyper-text transfer protocol secure, providing encrypted communication and secure identification of a web server.

You'll see URLs beginning with https where people want a higher level of security for ecommerce or financial transactions, or where sensitive data are passed back and forth. But you almost never have to say it. Most current browsers on domestic networks know how to display an https web page, like an http web page, just from the name and extension of the URL.

The Right Side of the Digital Divide

The problem is, just like Murray, you don't know what you don't know. Not you personally – anyone. If you walk into a business meeting with a three-year-old mobile device and you put it on the table, like so many of the digerati do, at some point someone is going to make a comment about it. It will be pejorative. Something like, "Nice phone," with a snarky, biting sarcasm that will make you want to rip the person's eyes out of their sockets. If you answer, "I'm waiting for the new ones to come out," your digital life is over. Remember, when you say something in a business meeting, you should be telling people what you know, not what you don't know. You can't say, "I'm waiting for the new ones to come out," because that answer tells the people in the room that you are completely out of the culture. If your phone is three years old, there have been 30 new phones introduced and end-of-lifed since you acquired it.

What should you have answered? "Are you kidding? This little phone saved my marriage. My wife, Bonnie, is so much happier with me now that I have given up my crackberry. Withdrawal took only two years ... although I'm still in therapy."

All kidding aside: you are defined by the clothes you wear, the beer you drink, the car you drive and the digital tools you carry. We'll talk more about this in a bit.

DIGITAL DICTIONARY

Digerati:
A play on the word glitterati
(glitter + literati) *which used to
describe the digital elite but has
become synonymous with the
less-laudable title of "geek."*

But before we do that, let's look at some short case studies. They are about completely fictitious individuals, but the situations described are all too real. Consider the following three job hunters:

Case Study: Invisible Irving

Irving is one of the most gifted chief financial officers in the world. He works for a multinational petrochemical conglomerate. The organization has fallen on hard times and his options are under water. Having worked in big corporate for almost 20 years, he is used to having all of his technology needs handled by the IT department. He has a BlackBerry, he uses Outlook on his laptop and everything is always in sync. He's never performed a backup of anything and, although he uses email all day long and searches Google like a madman, he really never thinks about computers or digital skills.

It's time to float his résumé, so he contacts a few headhunter friends, and they all agree to help. He has a professional service help him with his résumé. It's impressive. Irving is afraid (for good reason) to put his business email on his résumé, so he uses his personal email address smartirving55@aol.com. This is not impressive. In fact, it's professionally suicidal. Irving's email address is telling prospective hiring managers that he is a digital tourist with no understanding of the culture and, worse, he was probably born in 1955.

But this doesn't begin to describe Irving's problem (don't worry; we'll cover the conventions of email and why cute email names are a very bad professional idea in, Chapter 3 "The Fundamental Elements of Digital Life".

After reading Irving's very impressive résumé, a prospective employer searches for him on Google. Nothing. LinkedIn? Nothing. Facebook? Nope. This guy is invisible. He's the best CFO for the job, but he has absolutely no online presence. Sure, his name and title show up on the official documents in the public record. After all, he's the CFO of a publicly traded company. But there's nothing else. A few random mentions in an article or two, no picture, no feature stories, no blog mentions, no Google authorities. ... After a few minutes, the hiring manager gives up. Irving must not be that good; he's invisible.

The lesson here is profound. You can be great at your job, but if your online reputation does not match your offline reputation, you are going to have serious trouble getting a new job in the 21st-century economy.

Case Study: Frozen-in-Time Fred

Fred works as a regional sales manager for a major musical instrument (MI) manufacturer. He decided to use some digital tools to help him with his business a few years ago. He was very excited by the idea of blogging, did a few podcasts, and built a rudimentary website from a template. But all of it felt like too much work, so he stopped updating it. Fred put his bio online and even listed himself with some specialty search engines. And, in what must have seemed like a moment of brilliance, Fred even put his résumé in (what he thought was) a private location on his website. But he didn't actually check to see if it was private. Oops.

Now, here's the sad part. Fred is an awesome sales manager. He is a guy any MI manufacturer would want. A natural born leader, Fred is an inquisitive, outside-the-box thinker. He has boundless energy and has never had a year without double-digit sales increases.

There's only one problem. When the hiring manager from his dream job searched for him online, the amount of crap that surfaced made him look mediocre. Fred's online presence was old and outdated and told his prospective employers (and his prospective clients) that he was not in tune with the way business is done nowadays.

Does your online reputation match your offline reputation?

The lesson here is exactly the same as the lesson we learned from Invisible Irving. If your online reputation does not match your offline reputation, you're going to be at a serious disadvantage in the 21st century.

Case Study: Suboptimal (but Search-Savvy) Sam

Sam is an extremely untalented general sales manager for a major market television station. He is a stellar example of the Peter Principle: he has risen to his level of incompetence. Not only is Sam incompetent with regard to his corporate duties, he only knows how to manage up and his staff simply hates him.

But – and this is a big, big but – Sam is an Internet monster. He has a perfect Facebook profile, an impressive LinkedIn profile, several Twitter accounts and a podcast about fly fishing, which he actually *is* good at. He even has a very solid and reasonably popular blog about it.

Sam is careful to make sure that he puts out a social media update about what he is doing and where he is during his business day. He even makes some fairly smart comments about the industry which dozens and occasionally hundreds of people comment about online.

When hiring managers or headhunters Google Sam, they don't see an incompetent GSM who is universally hated by his staff; they see a textbook-perfect digital portrait of a contemporary, digitally savvy professional. Welcome to the 21st century.

The Online and Offline You

As you can see from our case studies, there is a startling disconnect between each person's offline and online presences. Invisible Irving would be a dream hire, but you'd never know it from your online search efforts. Frozen-in-Time Fred would also be a dream hire, but the results of his search tell the world that he ceased being digitally relevant years ago.

As bad as things are for Invisible Irving and Frozen-in-Time Fred, the good news is that both of them can use the tools and technologies described in this book to make their online and offline presences match.

The most unfortunate issue we have to deal with in the information age is Suboptimal (but search-savvy) Sam. He is the reason your online presence *has* to match your offline presence. In order to beat Sam, you have to be considered for the same opportunity. That can happen only if your digital presence is as good as or better than his. Why? Because everyone who wants to work with you or hire you starts by searching you on Google, Facebook and LinkedIn, pretty much in that order, and what everyone finds is instantly forged into a lasting first impression.

Your online presence has to match your offline presence. It is axiomatic in the information age. That sounds great, and it's relatively easy to accomplish (I promise). But what are you selling? Who are you? What are you? How should you think about your personal brand?

Chapter 2: Brand You

You Are a Bag of Doritos

Imagine you are walking down a grocery aisle. Bright, industrial lights splay down on a legion of nourishing choices. Opting instead to enjoy yourself, you head down the snack aisle. In about seven seconds you reach for a bag of Cool Ranch Doritos. The average American sees over 3,000 brand images each day, so making this choice feels pretty routine, but the big computer processor in your head goes through an amazingly complex set of choices before that bag hits your cart.

Want something salty or sweet? Chips, pretzels, popcorn or cheese puffs? Maybe go organic or low-fat? Save some coin with the generic brand or go for the good stuff? Ruffles, Pringles, Utz, Lays, Fritos or Doritos? Go with a favorite flavor like Nacho Cheese or Cool Ranch or try something new like Buffalo Wing or Guacamole? Should you pick up the fun size bags or a regular package or get the "family" serving? Obviously, this kind of multivariable decision making isn't conscious – that would be paralyzing. Rather, we've adapted to a more instinctual, subliminal assessment when faced with these kinds of overwhelming options.

This represents the challenge every marketer faces: how to cut through the clutter of a litany of choices. To survive in the digital age, you need to start thinking of yourself as that bag of Doritos. To hiring managers, potential clients and casual colleagues, you are a vaguely defined widget among many. It is your responsibility to stand out from the crowd, to define Brand You.

The idea of building a personal brand first appeared in a 1997 article[1] by Tom Peters in *Fast Company* magazine, but it has since reached critical mass. Selling yourself is nothing new. Ever since the bottom fell out on the Boomers, the hiring pool started looking more like the free-agency market of a professional sporting league than a dyed-in-the-wool marriage proposal between company and

[1] http://www.fastcompany.com/magazine/10/brandyou.html

employee. You were no longer an IBMer, but a Technology Product Manager, available to the highest bidder.

Today, tying your personal brand to a job title is about as useful as trying to sell a plain gray package with only the word "chips" printed on the front.

Your Personal Brand

Crafting a personal brand is about trumpeting benefits, not features. What unique perspectives do you have? What passions keep you up at night? What part of your personality draws people to you? An effective personal brand is a quip on where "what you do" meets "who you are." Think about what makes you different and how to present that to the world. Write this down in 15 words or less. If this elevator bio won't spark the interest of a stranger, delight potential clients and energize you to better yourself, you have a major problem. We've included some favorite personal brands of friends and colleagues to get you thinking in the right direction.

Brand You must be deliberated and executed with the same thoughtfulness and precision as the Fortune 500. Unfortunately, even if this is the first you've thought of a personal brand, you've been communicating your own for some time. All of us communicate a brand every day, not just by words, but by the clothes we wear, the jewelry we flash and the cars we drive. If someone were to plop down next to you at the bar and order a Budweiser, that person would be communicating a certain message. Ordering a glass of Chablis would convey a wholly different message. Fair or not, conscious or not, we all make and judge quick signals like this every day. Every single person reading this book exhibits a collection of symbols and habits that tell the world "This is who I am."

This offline collection is generally intentional and only broadcast to those in physical proximity. Our online collection is equally (and increasingly) socially important, naked to the entire world, constantly available and subject to forces beyond our control.

Offline vs. Online Brands

In certain ways this online collection is quite similar to an offline one. Above all, it's another shorthand system human beings use to comprehend the world around them. Quick judgments are formed from a variety of sources to form conscious decisions, often from subconscious questions: Is he like me and my friends? Is this what I'd expect an executive to look like? Have I had a bad experience with a person like this before? Paradoxically, the answers to these questions should be incredibly subjective, but they aren't. A well-defined personal brand, supporting a strong personal business plan, will include a specific set of digital symbols. Without the right digital symbols, you're invisible; with the wrong ones, you're a liability.

In other ways, an online collection is dramatically different from an offline one. Worryingly, and most importantly, an online brand is not entirely within your control. Every online-capable person in the world has access to you and your work, even when you're asleep. There are strategies to massage search results, tactics to limit embarrassing information and a set of tools and toys that communicate being "with it," but at a certain point, once something is on the web, there is a limit to available damage control. To put it a bit more bluntly, there is no "undo" button on an uploaded sex tape.

Baratunde Thurston
Job: Web Managing Editor, The Onion
Personal Brand: Conscious Comic and Vigilante Pundit

Richard Sellers
Job: Marketing Executive
Personal Brand: Transformer of Marketing Budgets to Profit

Shelly Palmer
Job: Technology, Media and Entertainment Consultant
Personal Brand: Digital Guru and Tech Therapist

Mike Raffensperger
Job: Vice President, Strategic and Creative Development
Personal Brand: Passionate Storyteller and Aspiring Digerati

As with all things on the web, these judgments are made faster and harsher. In an offline setting, you can recover from a faux pas or reverse a first impression. In an online setting, you're probably unaware when someone is sizing you up. If a person doesn't find something appealing after 20 seconds with Google, that's it. No second chances.

So, how *can* an online brand be controlled? In a way, this entire book is about building your digital identity. The topics and tactics you'll learn are part of the ingrained digital culture. As you overcome the digital divide, you will start to understand what parts to make your own, ignore and add to. The personal brand of a creative director will look different from that of a sales manager. That said, there are some basic guidelines within digital life you can use as groundcover for your personal brand, which we will review in the next chapter.

Branding Benchmarks

Before diving in, however, it's important that you get your digital bearings. The most popular metric for gauging an individual's online presence is easily Google. Google yourself. Right now. It's not vain; it's a vital aspect of online persona and professional management. If no results, or worse yet, the wrong results, appear in a Google search for your name, you are setting yourself up for digital disaster. On the other hand, having the right results appear is the digital equivalent of being at the right cocktail parties, speaking on the right panels and being mentioned in the right boardrooms. For success in the digital age, you simply must master your Google presence.

DIGITAL DICTIONARY

Egosurf:

A colloquialism for performing and investigating a Google search on one's own name.

Now, Google the names of a few of the biggest individuals in your field. By benchmarking yourself against others in your field, you'll discover things they do well and things they do poorly. More importantly, you'll get a feel for the results that impress you. An ideal egosurf will return a huge number of results displaying interviews with various online outlets, hosted podcasts, online video productions, an engaging blog, press release quotes, listed speaking engagements, recorded webinars, awards won and a robust network of online profiles and memberships.

Chapter 3: The Fundamental Elements of Digital Life

We've discussed the importance of getting a handle on your digital life, and by this point you should understand the consequences of embracing your digital life or ignoring it. You should appreciate the unique value of establishing a strong personal brand and building that brand with purpose and diligence. And at a basic level, you should grasp the landscape used to judge and measure digital credence.

This is a good beginning. But to truly become more successful, you'll need not just to acknowledge but also to actively manage each element of your digital life, the pieces that fit together to fill out your digital puzzle. This chapter will outline, and review in brief, the primary elements of digital life. If you don't fully understand all that is being said in this chapter, don't worry. This is only the basics and a checklist to reference later. Most elements in this chapter will receive more attention and greater detail later in the book.

Email

One of the most visible elements of digital life is an email address. While it's an increasingly irrelevant medium to teens (who are far more likely to text or use social networks for day-to-day communication), it is, and will remain, a critical method of communication to the adult working world. Over a considerable period of time it may become outmoded, but for the foreseeable future, email is here to stay. Every living person should maintain no less than four separate addresses.

Your Professional or Work Email

The first is a professional address through which all your professional correspondence channels. Follow your employer's naming conventions or simply use your first and last name, and always follow the @ sign with a company name. In a perfect world, you will have your own domain name, for example, companyname.com or shellypalmer.com. Then your professional email could be shelly.palmer@companyname.com or shelly@shellypalmer.com – both are best practices examples.

DIGITAL DICTIONARY

Domain:

The part of website URLs you recognize. Domains are broken into two parts, the hostname and the top-level domain. The hostname is the unique bit – the google in google.com and the wikipedia in wikipedia.org. The top-level domain is the suffix after the hostname. Examples of top-level domains include .com, .org, .info and .edu. Top-level domains generally refer to online verticals and offer a cursory understanding of a website's purpose. The .com sites are for commercial purposes, .org sites are for nonprofit organizations, .info is for information-based websites and .edu indicates official educational facilities. Most top-level domains are not strictly regulated (though some, like .gov and .edu, are) but can generally be used as an accurate representation of a site's content.

Of course, it is very hard to get proper names as domain names nowadays; almost every combination of words in the English language has already been purchased.

The other option, workable but far less desirable, is to create a Gmail account using your first and last name, for example, shelly.palmer@gmail.com. This is reasonably professional and acceptable as an "in the culture" email address. However – and I can't stress this enough – a professional email address that is not at a custom domain name or a business name says to the recipient, "This person does not work for a digitally savvy business and does not have enough digital skill to register a custom domain name."

In short, it says you are on the wrong side of the digital divide.

If at all possible, save Gmail for your personal address.

Your Personal Email

Your personal address should also simply be your first and last name or a simple variation of such. Don't get too cute with your name; yes, this is a personal account, but it's one you'll use to pay your bills, submit résumés and interact with the reputable adult world. It's hard to take someone named SweetCheeks73 seriously.

As I already mentioned, Gmail, Google's free online mail service, is a great option for a personal email address. Gmail has the best feature set of any online mail service – virtually unlimited space, threaded reply display, searchable mail, filtering and labeling – but there is a much more important reason to use it. Gmail is the service of choice for those in the know. And to those in the know, using a service like hotmail or yahoo appears out of touch. Make no mistake: the three deadliest letters in digital life are A-O-L.

If your name is not available on gmail, and at this point it may not be, then try to find an easily readable variation, for example, spalmer@gmail.com, s.palmer@gmail.com, and so on. If all else fails, create something using your name and location or name and profession, for example, shellypalmerny@gmail.com.

Your Super Secret Email

The third account everyone should have is an ultrapersonal, super-secret email address. This should be named something cryptic and unrelated to your actual name. This address should be shared only with those close to you. Do with it as you wish (I won't ask). That said, no matter how cryptic the email handle, it's easily traceable back to the computer it's sent from. By extension, it is traceable back to you. The confidentiality this email provides is fairly superficial, so don't do anything stupid; divorce lawyers will easily find and subpoena it.

Regardless, you owe it to yourself to have a very private email account to handle your ultraprivate online activity.

Your Junk Email

The fourth email address you need is a junk email or spam account. It doesn't really matter what this is or who hosts it; just use it anytime you're forced to submit an email address but don't really trust the organization asking for it. As a rule of thumb, if something free on the web is asking for an email address, pass them the spam account. You can always change it to one of your other addresses later.

With 90% of all the world's email qualifying as spam[2], it's vital to guard genuine accounts from disreputable sources. Even the best spam filters miss some solicitations, and having a dummy account to deflect most of them is a real productivity saver.

Website

One of the simplest ways to build and protect a digital brand is operating your own website. Services like Media Temple, 1&1 and GoDaddy are incredibly easy

[2]http://www.pcworld.com/article/165533/90_percent_of_email_is_spam_symantec_says.html

to use, and domain registration costs are remarkably inexpensive. Even if you don't have the time or interest to run a website right now, you should register a domain of your first and last name. Domains are like real estate on the web. Even if you only "squat" on the property for the time being, it's important to stake out turf to protect.

After you register a domain, your website needs a host and content management system to function. There are worlds of options available for both of these services, ranging from feature-lacking and free to feature-rich and costly. For current recommendations and resources on how to establish a functional website, visit www.OvercomingTheDigitalDivide.com.

Blog

One of the most powerful ways to establish online identity is authoring a blog. Blogs enjoy a nearly ubiquitous presence on the web, with over hundreds of millions of registered blogs currently in existence. Most people are aware of what a blog is: an authored set of chronologically listed entries. It's important here to differentiate between blogs and websites. Think back to geometry class: squares are rectangles, but rectangles are not squares. In a similar vein, all blogs are websites, but not all websites are blogs. Philosophically, a website can be relatively static, perhaps only including your bio, contact information and accomplishments, while a blog is a regularly updated, much more fluid medium. Technically, a blog is simply a specific type of website, usually supported by a content management system (CMS) designed for a nontechnical user featuring what-you-see-is-what-you-get publishing tools.

Why would anyone want to blog? A fresh, compelling and popular blog is one of the single most effective ways to establish a digital presence. Because of their frequently updated nature and inclination to receive and send links to other bloggers, blogs are naturally viral and rank well with Google (more on this later). Besides, they're fun! People blog for all kinds of reasons: personal passion, profitability, curiosity or professional ambition. Some blogs resemble a series of feature-like articles, while others are short, pithy bits of commentary. Most are primarily text, but many use photography, video, audio or a mix of media. All that matters is to decide why to blog, stick with the theme, and keep it *regularly* updated. There is nothing more useless to a reader and terrible for your image than an abandoned blog that hasn't seen an update in months. Don't feel like each and every entry needs to be perfect prose housing your utmost brilliance.

A couple of hundred words and a picture, regularly added on a daily basis, are almost always more valuable than intermittent essays to author and audience both. For fresh resources on the what, why and how of starting a blog, visit www. OvercomingTheDigitalDivide.com.

Social Media

Social media platforms share a lot of similarities with blogs: they're ubiquitous, effective personal brand purveyors, and they require a strategy. In order for that strategy to work, it's critical that you understand the culture of consumption within each network and adhere to its norms. Would you pass out business cards at a funeral or drink car bombs at a business meeting? No? Then pay attention.

LinkedIn

Arguably, LinkedIn is the most important network for professionals. This is not a place for friends; it's a place for business, and only business. In the digital age, it is essential to create and fully complete a LinkedIn profile. Be comprehensive and craft a flattering professional narrative, but do *not* pad this CV. The truth has a particularly poignant way of coming to light on the web. Concisely add the fullest appropriate work history, education and other résumé information, with your most recent experience listed at the top of your profile.

The network tends to be more static than others with fewer status updates, messages and discussion flying back and forth. However, LinkedIn does have certain unique passive and professional benefits, enabling users to find and foster contacts with connections of connections, public group discussions around every professional topic imaginable, job boards with great features for job seeker and employer alike, advanced search functionality for fairly robust data mining and in-vertical Q&A functions. For the latest tips and techniques for LinkedIn, visit www.OvercomingTheDigitalDivide.com.

Cautionary Note: You can easily configure your LinkedIn, Facebook and Twitter profiles so that one status update (Tweet) is immediately and automatically distributed to all three social networks. Does it make sense for your old high school friends to see a tweet you have just crafted about your business?

Facebook

Facebook is the big boy on the block. With over hundreds of millions of active users[3], Facebook is a nation unto itself, and that's why resistance is futile. There is no option but to be on Facebook. In the same way email and cell phones were once considered secondary channels and are now essential to everyday communication, Facebook is a required contact touch point.

DIGITAL DICTIONARY

Micro-celebrity:

The web-centric phenomenon of being extremely well known to a group of people. The number of followers can be very small (e.g., the foodie within a circle of friends) to relatively large (e.g., A-list bloggers, Internet executives and web-show stars).

If you have not already done so, create an account. Use your real name and a real photograph; the entire utility of the tool depends on an honest representation. Use it to foster micro-celebrity, interface with professional contacts or intimately engage with friends and family. Just be sure to pick a strategy – know why you're there and whom you're friends with. Generally, it's not a great idea to allow worlds to mingle. Your CFO doesn't need to see candids from your last Vegas trip, and your old college roommates don't need a floor update from the industry expo.

Generally, I recommend choosing which type of profile you're going to adopt and pruning your network to match it. However, for those who want to split the difference, I strongly recommend against creating two different profiles; that's confusing for everyone involved. Instead, use the Facebook feature called Lists. In this way you can create different groups within your Facebook network. Divide your network into lists that you want to separate access for – perhaps family, friends and professional contacts.

Once that is complete, go to your Privacy Settings under the Account tab. From there you can customize who is able to see any type of content on your Facebook profile. For example, you might want to make Photos and Videos I'm Tagged In viewable by Friends Only while your Status Updates are viewable by Everyone.

Personalities of note may want to consider creating a fan page instead of a personal profile. A fan page is generally used by businesses, brands, celebrities

[3]http://www.facebook.com/press/info.php?statistics

and other entities that require a more robust method of interacting with the Facebook community. Not sure if you should make a personal profile or a fan page? For the vast majority of people, a personal profile is the way to go; however, if you believe you'll foster over 5,000 connections on Facebook, consider creating a fan page; personal profiles are limited to 5,000 "friends."

Regardless, never publish incriminating, embarrassing or unflattering content on Facebook. Yes, privacy settings are available. Yes, you can curate who is a part of your network. And yes, you can remove indiscreet posts. But, and this cannot be stressed enough, there is no reasonable expectation of privacy online. If something could result in your arrest, firing or divorce, it really goes without saying: don't post it! For the latest tips and techniques for Facebook, visit www. OvercomingTheDigitalDivide.com.

Twitter

Twitter is often described as "the conversation happening right now." Of course, that's overly simplistic.

Twitter represents a communication paradigm shift. Twitter is a real-time, public stream that can be parsed, shared and contributed to by anyone. Perhaps more so than any other social media tool, you get out of Twitter what you put into it. Can it be an inane stream of pointless lifecasting ("The line at Starbucks is soooo LONG!")? Yes. But by focusing on following and fostering connections with a purpose, Twitter can create an ambient awareness that's truly unlike any other source of information. It's like a stock ticker, but instead of quantitative market information, it provides real-time qualitative information on anything and everything. And as much as Twitter is an opportunity to listen, it is also a chance to be heard. Twitter is by definition a micro-blog: a series of short, chronological updates. Use it just as you would a blog to build a personal brand, and you'll be on the right track to getting the most out of Twitter.

For the time being, it is a very good idea to register an account, even if only to reserve the most desirable version of your name available. Start following the publications and personalities you find valuable and get a feel for how people exchange on the network. Specifically, notice how users will include the @ symbol followed by another username as a form of mentioning or replying to each other.

 Sometimes, users will include the letters RT and @ username in their tweet. This is an abbreviation for retweet and indicates that the user is circulating a

message originally published by someone else. This is one of the key Twitter currencies: people *love* being retweeted. It's flattering and the primary way users communicate with people outside their own followers. For the latest Twitter tips and techniques, visit www.OvercomingTheDigitalDivide.com.

MySpace

Ah, MySpace. Once the undisputed king of social networks, now ghettoized into a doddering asylum of digital juveniles, nefarious scam artists and 40-year-old men pretending to be teenagers. I suppose it should go without saying that it's not particularly important to maintain an account on MySpace. As a communication vehicle, MySpace is a failure. However, as a content distribution vehicle, it's an important player, especially for the music business. If you are a content producer, consider utilizing MySpace to promote and distribute your creations.

Wikipedia

Wikipedia is the encyclopedia of choice for any digital native. Some argue it is an unreliable source of information, citing the fact that anyone can edit the site's content. While technically true, this argument exposes a lack of understanding of how the site effectively works. A number of vandalism safeguards exist, and an army of volunteer editors do a surprisingly excellent job of keeping the site accurate. In an independent study[4] by *Nature*, an anonymous sampling of a variety of articles from both Wikipedia and *The Encyclopedia Britannica* was submitted to a group of experts for peer review. The results of their review found similar levels of factual accuracy in both Wikipedia and *Britannica*. No one suggests taking Wikipedia (or any other single source) as gospel, but it's a fantastic jumping-off point for an enormous breadth of topics.

Hopefully, one of those topics includes you or your work, but don't create an article on yourself, your company or your product just yet – Wikipedia generally discourages this as a conflict of interest. An individual must meet notability requirements for an entry to remain published. For more information on these requirements, visit http://en.wikipedia.org/wiki/Wikipedia:Notability.

If you feel you meet these requirements, search for yourself on Wikipedia. If an entry exists, ensure the information is accurate and complete. If no entry exists, it's probably not a good idea to create one. As a rule of thumb, new articles are expected to make Wikipedia, not individual egos, more comprehensive.

---

[4] http://news.cnet.com/Study-Wikipedia-as-accurate-as-Britannica/2100-1038_3-5997332.html

Specialized Portals

For some, inclusion in specialized or professional portals is a vital aspect of personal online visibility. Those working in show business should be listed on IMDB. High-society socialites, jet-setters and other masters of the universe may consider trying to break into the exclusive online network A Small World.[5] Journalists and expert sources might consider participating in the Help a Reporter Out[6] network. Investigate your industry on Google and ask colleagues if they know of influential online destinations.

For fresh tips on how to get the most out of social media, visit www.OvercomingTheDigitalDivide.com.

Instant Message (IM)

Instant messaging services, such as AOL IM, Yahoo Messenger, gchat and iChat, can be extremely useful for day-to-day communication. They can be a great way to grab a quick answer from a colleague, easily send a file for client review or make last-minute dinner plans with friends. It's a unique communication hybrid, pairing the convenience and low-pressure nature of email with the immediacy and reciprocity of a phone call.

To get started, choose which instant message service you'd like to use. I recommend AIM (www.aim.com), as it is very popular and shares its user network with Google and Apple's IM software iChat, which comes preloaded with every new Apple computer. Simply head to the software's site, download the client, install it on your computer and set up an account. As with your personal email, choose an instant message username that won't be embarrassing to share with clients and colleagues.

That said, there is a school of thought that espouses the virtues of a very, very cryptic IM name to reduce or eliminate random or unwanted chat buddies. Not for nothing, my IM name is cryptic. I never want anyone to IM me unless I invite that person to do so.

---

[5] www.asmallworld.net
[6] www.helpareporter.com

Skype

Skype[7] is a fantastic online service that allows conversation over an Internet connection rather than a phone line. Skype provides two primary benefits over a traditional phone conversation: international calls and video chat capabilities. Calling internationally or using a cell phone overseas can rack up monstrous charges. Skype is free or, in the cases where they do charge for calls, very low cost. Additionally, with a webcam-equipped computer, it's easy to set up a video teleconference with anyone in the world – all you need is an Internet connection.

In some regards, Skype works similarly to Instant Message services. You can text, talk and video chat with other users on the service for free. To place an actual phone call, however, you will need to deposit credits, which are charged on a (very reasonable) per-minute basis. To get started, just go to www.skype.com, then download, install and set up the client.

Unlike my IM name, my Skype name is super easy to find and understand. It's "shellypalmerny." While it's true that Skype and IM share common characteristics, I treat Skype like a phone system and an associated phone directory. I want my international clients and colleagues to be able to call me for free or for super-low rates. And I am diligent about setting my status on Skype when I'm not available for a call or chat.

Cell Phone

Mobile phones occupy the strange space in which the offline and online worlds collide. Mobile phones are both incredibly useful digital tools and modern-day six-shooters that cowboy executives plop on conference tables to announce, "I am important, busy and connected." Without question, having a modern, modish smartphone is an important brand symbol, but smartphones also genuinely shift the way everyday life is managed. At this point, it is simply and absolutely necessary to own a smartphone, and it should be an iPhone, Android, BlackBerry or Windows Phone.

Most corporations that provide smartphones for their employees use Research in Motion's BlackBerry. It plays nicer with IT departments, has good

[7]www.skype

email functionality and its physical keyboard is considered a necessity for rapid-fire typing for some. While BlackBerry has been the de facto business mobile workhorse, users appear to be ditching the platform in droves. The visual appeal, robust app market and increasing corporate adoption of the iPhone and Android are major threats to the BlackBerry's supremacy.

Frankly, this makes sense. The iPhone is one of the sexiest devices ever to grace the planet, and it touts a competitive advantage its contemporaries are unlikely to fully replicate: the App Store. Independent developers can create and distribute third-party applications through the iPhone's App Store. These applications transform the iPhone from a relatively static smartphone to almost anything needed or desired. Want a visual sign language dictionary? There's an app for that. Want to remotely monitor an ER patient's vital signs? There's an app for that. Want an ultrasonic bug zapper? Well, you get the idea.

Other companies have opened their own app markets, but thanks to Apple's marketing savvy and sex appeal, they have enticed thousands of developers to create hundreds of thousands of apps. The more applications available, the more attractive the platform is to consumers, and the more consumers using the platform, the more attractive it becomes to developers.

That said, Google's Android platform is more than twice as popular as Apple's iOS, and Android phones are available from multiple carriers. Android is not actually hardware in and of itself; it's only the operating system that handset makers construct their mobile devices around. Because many manufacturers use the Android Operating System (OS) on their devices (only Apple iPhones use Apple's iOS operating system), phones and devices that run Android outnumber other types of devices. Android's greatest strength – its open, "do-everything" app market and operating system – may also be its Achilles heel. One of the key differences between the Android and iPhone platforms is the Android's open, developer-friendly application market. Unlike Apple's byzantine and arguably tyrannical way of working with app developers (they've been known to ban applications for questionable reasons, and the application submission process is universally hated by developers), Android developers

DIGITAL DICTIONARY

OS (operating system):

A piece of software that provides the user interface environment in which other software runs. The most famous example of an OS is Windows, but all modern pieces of computing hardware have some form of OS running on them.

are free to construct applications that act in any way they wish.

At face value, this seems like an obvious, objective good. There are drawbacks. User interfaces vary greatly from application to application on Android phones. They are uniformly simple and efficient on an iPhone. Beyond these usability issues, the more lax app approval process on the Android market leaves it more vulnerable to viruses and malware.

Long story short, which one should you buy? If you work for a corporation and always plan to, use whatever your company gives you for business and get an iPhone or an Android for pleasure. If you work for yourself and are technologically conservative, really want a physical keyboard or are a heavy email user, get a BlackBerry. In-the-middle, media consumers who want an always useful, flexible mobile should get an iPhone or Android. Tech geeks or people who want ultimate control and complete freedom should get an Android. And gamers who live and die on Xbox should consider a Windows Phone – the integration with Windows is truly extraordinary.

Google

Google is ludicrously important – so much so, the entire next chapter is dedicated to it. At this point, simply understand that how you appear in Google, both in terms of the number and relevancy of search results, is *very* important.

Hardware

The Joneses treadmill of the digital age, keeping your hardware current, is an ongoing and never-ending element of digital life. While your clients' and colleagues' expectation that you are staying up to date is important, it's more important that you stay up to date for your own sake. What's more, hardware advances at a blinding pace. A useful concept to keep in mind when shopping and replacing hardware is Moore's Law. Attributed to the observation of Intel cofounder Gordon Moore, Moore's Law suggested that the density of semiconductors on a silicon chip would double every 18 months. People with less knowledge of how the electronics industry works extended Moore's Law to cover everything from the speed of processors to the size of memory chips to the capacities of hard drives. It turns out Mr. Moore was wrong. Nowadays, sizes double about every six months, and the pace of innovation is accelerating.

Why do you care? Within a couple of years, that brand-new, top-tier system you just purchased will be a sluggish, cringe-worthy relic.

Just don't go overboard! Very few professionals truly need top-of-the-line digital and computing hardware. People who run out to buy the newest, latest and greatest are known as early adopters. While it can be tremendous fun to be the first to experience new technology, adopting early usually entails paying a huge premium for a device with technical flaws. Those flaws occasionally result in the abandonment of the device as a priority by its manufacturer, or more likely, the release of a cheaper, better version shortly down the line. Most people don't find early adoption an enjoyable experience on the whole.

It's likely you simply need to replace your computer every few years with a decent upgrade and strive to keep your servers, cameras, displays and other digital equipment current enough to perform at above-average levels.

Laptop or Desktop, Tablet or eReader, Netbook or Smartphone?

Each part of this question has a personal answer, an economic answer and a professional answer. Do you need an iPad? Do you need a Kindle? Do you need a Mac Pro Desktop with dual 30" monitors? If you know that you need any of these devices, you already have them. If you are unsure, we'll cover the must haves in detail in Chapter 8.

But basically, this question is often answered in the same manner in which you got dressed this morning: you decided what to wear based on the activities you were going to do. If you were going on an important interview, you would put on your best clothes, fix your hair, and so on. Would it help you to walk into that meeting with an iPad as opposed to a laptop or a netbook? In many cases, it's not the features of the devices that matter, it's the perceived benefits of ownership.

Software

The best hardware in the world is worthless if it doesn't have someone operating it with the right software knowhow. Every working professional of the digital age is required to have baseline skill with certain software. There are no excuses on this one. Before long, not having these skills will feel akin to being an executive who doesn't type: archaic, astounding and a bit sad. In the meantime, having someone else complete these tasks is inefficient and often impractical.

- **Advanced Google.** There is no way around this one; you must be great at using Google. You must know how to search using specialized parameters. You should be able to find only results published in the past 24 hours, who is linking to your recent blog post, all the sites that published your recent press quote, exact and entire phrases (not just keywords), all the web pages that include your name but not your company name and many other advanced search techniques. For a good list and series of videos with some great Google tips and tricks, visit www.OvercomingTheDigitalDivide.com.

- **Advanced Microsoft Office.** Specifically, this includes Outlook, Word, Excel and PowerPoint. If you don't understand how to request a meeting in Outlook, use Track Changes in Word, create formulas in Excel or set up slide transitions in PowerPoint, you're in trouble. Take the time to learn these programs by searching online for tutorials, using the program's Help function or simple trial and error or taking a class. Understanding these programs is nonnegotiable for the modern businessperson.

- **Basic HTML.** You don't need to be able to code a website from scratch, but you should have a basic familiarity with the computer coding language HTML. While it may not seem like "computer programming" in and of itself, a basic understanding of HTML is a requisite for intelligent navigation of the web. Can you determine what keywords your competitors are using in the View Source function on your web browser? Can you italicize, bold and underline the comments you make on web blogs? Can you converse intelligently with your web design and development team about basic needs and tasks? Can you use an "href" to place an image on a webpage? If not, I promise you, there are plenty of upstarts fresh out of college who can. Don't worry about this now; I'll show you some important basics later.

- **Basic photo editing.** Images and photographs are an undeniably powerful form of communication. They push any piece of digital content to the next level. They demand attention. As such, you must be able to manipulate them, even if only in the most basic manner. With either a full-featured program like Photoshop or a free program like Picasa or GIMP, you should be able to crop, resize, add text, adjust resolutions, remove blemishes, add filtered effects and generally improve the quality of any image

- **Basic video editing.** If an image is worth a thousand words, what is a moving image worth? Regardless, the person able to manipulate that video is worth a lot. You don't need to be able to re-create Michael Bay–inspired special effects or put a story together with the artfulness of Steven Spielberg, but you should be able to cut together basic highlights, add text and generally pace video material that will satisfy and engage its audience. For the vast majority of people, Apple's iMovie or Windows' Movie Maker will more than suffice for basic video editing needs. Conveniently, these come prepackaged with either operating system, and there are about a billion videos on YouTube showing you how to do exactly what you want.

Chapter 4:
The Currency of the Web

One of the main goals of this book is to help you translate the value of your intellectual property into wealth. We are very used to translating the value of our intellectual property into cash. If someone pays you to do a job, you are translating the value of what you know how to do (your intellectual property) into cash, which in this case is a measure of wealth.

As easy as this is to do in the offline world, it is really tough to do online. It's relatively easy to create something of value online. AOL IM is very valuable, but it does not directly make any money for AOL. YouTube is very valuable, but if it were not owned by Google, it could not afford its bandwidth bill. There are literally millions of websites that will pirate music or video or help you code or create something, but they do not and cannot be used to directly translate their value into wealth.

This is where the other currencies of the web come in. Let's have a look at some of the most popular forms of online currency and see how we might use them to translate value into wealth.

Information

Information, specifically exclusive and filtered information, is a currency. Imagine a cab driver on West 38th Street in Midtown Manhattan driving aimlessly, looking for a fare. If he had a device in his cab that told him there was a fare waiting on 38th and Lex, he could almost immediately translate that information into cash. If several cabs had that information, it would be less valuable. If every cab had that information, it would simply be a business methodology with only commodity value. Any Wall Streeter will tell you that information (especially exclusive information) is cash. But a person living in the suburbs with knowledge of a sale at a local store can translate that information into cash just as easily.

The web is simply a giant pool of information. Information on pet grooming, the geopolitical climate of Uzbekistan, the phone number of your local deli, what your sister is doing this weekend – anything and everything. Many people create and monetize blogs solely on the basis of sharing and explaining specialized information. Connecting questions with answers is one of the web's specialties.

What information do you have that could translate into cash?

Attention

Attention is such an established currency, it's written into the grammar of the English language: you "pay" and "receive" attention. Any sitting president knows well the currency of attention. Using the bully pulpit, he can sway voters, move Congress to enact legislation or cow foreign powers to cease hostilities. Nearly the entire business model of broadcast television is built on attention; it packages the attention of its audience and sells it to sponsors.

But you need not be a master of the universe to translate attention into wealth. In 1995, Craig Newmark started a simple email list among friends, announcing social events of interest to software developers living in the San Francisco Bay area. Subscribers and the number of event postings grew rapidly. Local employers began posting available development jobs to the list, and soon Craig saw an explosive demand for additional categories and a web interface. You likely now know this website as craigslist.org. It's more than a success story. Take a few moments and Wiki it.

Trust Circles

In the digital age, each of us commands a sphere of influence, holding the ear of any number of people, our own personal circle of trust. There is someone reading this sentence right now who with a single email could drive dozens of people to a musical performance, restaurant opening, volleyball game, fashion sale, classic car show, art exhibit, civic protest or just about anything under the sun.

Whose attention do you command?

Intention

Sometimes it's not what you said; it's what you meant. This is called intention. Google translates the currency of intention into several billions of dollars each year. They know that when you come to Google, your intention is to find something. They delight in telling you that in .02 seconds, they have found 2,374,345 things that you may have intended to click on. They offer all of their services for free. Why? They know that if they pay off your intention with valuable information, you will keep coming back, and they assume that if you show up often enough, you might click on something they get paid for. And you do. We all do. A lot. It's the best currency of intention to cash money translation engine ever created.

While you may not operate one of the world's most successful online services, you can extract tremendous value simply by understanding what your audience intends to find. That audience may be customers using your e-shopping cart, readers of your blog or simply friends on your Facebook profile. Regardless, understanding why your audience is there and what they intend to find is essential.

Often, this currency is in play when designing and developing websites. There's a saying, "If you ask the wrong question, you're guaranteed to get the wrong answer." The question I get asked all the time is, "How do you like the look of our site?" Who cares! The proper question is, "What do our users expect our site to do and, when they visit the site, do we satisfy their expectations?" The proper question is not, "What do you think of our website?" The proper question is, "Has the site met or exceeded its conversion goals, or have you been able to measure and profitably package your audience for yourself or for your clients?"

Are you identifying audience intentions and delivering on their expectations?

Fame

"In the future everybody will be world famous for fifteen minutes."
—Andy Warhol

Andy's famous prediction has long since come true. Everyone with an Internet-connected device has access to a global publishing platform, to say nothing of reality television and man-on-the-street interviews for *The Late Show*. All kidding aside, we often take for granted the incredible content creation and distribution tools at our disposal. Anyone with Microsoft Word and an Amazon CreateSpace account can publish, print and distribute a book nearly as effectively as those working with a traditional publishing house. Aspiring filmmakers once required expensive equipment, specialized training and cooperation from the studio cabal. Dedicated creatives are now perfectly capable of producing a similar result with a handheld digital camera, a laptop computer and an Internet connection. Many bloggers regularly attract greater readership than nationally syndicated newspaper columnists. The truth is that in the digital age, fame is simply a function of talent, desire and drive.

The ability of fame to turn itself into cash is astounding. Perhaps you won't be able to pull a LeBron James–inspired multimillion-dollar endorsement deal, but some companies may be willing to compensate you for positive association. The Academy Awards may not be asking you to host next year, but you might work out a speaking fee at your industry's upcoming conference and expo. You can leverage fame with everything from paid commentary writing to the merchandising of your personal brand. The opportunities and extent to which you wish to do so are entirely up to you.

What do people know you for?

Passion

Genuine passion is irresistible, intoxicating and contagious. We all cherish the individuals in our lives who possess seemingly unending energy and enthusiasm. They better themselves and better those around them purely through force of will.

Gary Vaynerchuk is one such individual. The son of Russian immigrants, he spent his summers working the cash register at his family's wine store in Springfield, New Jersey. As a teenager, he became enamored with the idea of refining his palate. Taking the only legal recourse available, Gary began tasting obscure fruits and vegetables, grass, dirt, rocks, tobacco and wood – all in an effort to study the various flavors associated with refined wine. Soon after college, Gary rebranded the family store as "The Wine Library," became the store's sole wine buyer and emerged as a trusted resource and guide for the area's wine lovers. Within a five-year period, the Wine Library grew annual revenue from $4 million to $45 million.

That is the least impressive part of Gary's story.

Driven by what he saw as the pretentious, unwelcoming atmosphere of professional wine critics, Gary created Wine Library TV, a web video show with an everyday attitude toward wine education. Gary often comes across more like a motivational speaker than a sommelier, offering cheeky commentary, zealous evangelism of wine and unconventional segments such as "What wine pairs with breakfast cereal?" His enthusiasm has earned him a cult-like following of thousands of daily viewers, launched his store to national recognition, garnered primetime television appearances and helped him become a *New York Times* Bestselling Author. He has since become one of the most influential wine critics in the United States.

What passion burns within you?

Respect

Arguably, respect is the most valuable of all the currencies of the web. Respect is earned. Always. Information can be learned, attention can be demanded, intention can be discovered, fame can be stumbled into and passion can come naturally. But respect is always earned, often through hard-fought, time-tested consistency. And that means people value you – not what you know or how you present yourself, but *you*. Treat this currency with care and it will become one of your most valuable resources.

What would it be worth to a recent MBA to have dinner with Jack Welch? What lengths would an aspiring filmmaker go to in order to be on-set next to Martin Scorsese? What quarterback wouldn't move heaven and earth to train with Peyton Manning? Respect is so valuable, it can be hard to quantify.

But you need not be a world-renowned celebrity to derive value from respect. If you've spent much time in your industry, you may be surprised at the number of colleagues, clients, superiors and subordinates you've impressed over the years. Reputations have a way of spreading, and you can leverage this (hopefully) good will in all types of ways. Fostering mentor/mentee relationships can reap rewards money can't buy. Selling consultancy services and commentary writing can be an excellent source of income. Accepting interview appearances and speaking opportunities translates respect into fame. Respect can do everything from garnering deference in a board meeting to ranking you higher in a Google search.

Manage it carefully, and this long-bearing fruit will serve you well.

Whose respect do you earn?

Translation Engines

A successful contemporary business model needs to translate the value of one currency into another. Our jobs now must include the creation and ongoing maintenance of translation engines designed to turn passion into profits, respect into attention, intention into attention and so on. The good news is that all of this can be done using digital tools and a little personal creativity. I could spend dozens of pages explaining how one might translate these various currencies into wealth, but you get the idea, and ultimately the way you do this will be unique to you – which is how it should be.

Chapter 5: Google

You Are Stupid

The holy grail of any marketing department is entrenching a brand so deeply in the minds of consumers, it's no longer a choice among many; it simply is. Do you eat gelatin or Jell-O? Use a BandAid or an adhesive bandage? Need a facial tissue, or reach for a Kleenex? Google is no longer a noun; it's a verb. People don't search; they Google. And this little branding coup is *meaningless* when compared to the effect Google had on our society and our economy.

In his book *The Dumbest Generation: How the Digital Age Stupefies Young Americans and Jeopardizes Our Future,* author Mark Bauerlein argues everyone under 30 is an intellectual retrograde. He laments high school and college classes full of ingrates who don't read the paper, can't spell and refuse to memorize the dates and facts of the Civil War. Mark's perspective makes sense. Retaining vast amounts of knowledge was at one time extremely valuable. Information, particularly obscure or specialized information, had hard value. By extension, a person with that information was valuable. But using his definition of intelligence, Mark is dumber than Google. So are you. So is every person on this planet.

What Mark fails to acknowledge is the new information economy, one that isn't based on knowledge retention, but on knowledge translation. It's about a digital shorthand that affords enormous digestion of information, and an ability to efficiently weed out the good and useful from the false and feckless. Mark is correct; very few digital natives read the paper. Instead, they regularly consume different blogs, papers and news feeds through an RSS reader in half the time it takes Mark to get through the Sunday *Times*. Digital natives are confident that their social networks will push uniquely germane information to them, instantly. They don't have to pull information out of a mostly irrelevant mess of pulp that was out of date before it went to print. A digital native doesn't worry about knowing when the Battle of Bull Run Bridge took place, because that information is readily available at his desk, on his smartphone and in his coffee shop, 24 hours a day, 7 days a week. In fact, Google was used six times just to write these few paragraphs. If you're curious, those six Google searches were "brand becomes vowel," "theasurous" (yes, that's how badly the spelling was butchered; Google still figured it out), "the dumbest generation," "famous civil war battles," "newsvine" and "recent Google searches." Took about 48 seconds.

However, while it is true that we live in the information age, remember: information is *not* knowledge! It's just a bunch of data points that need to be contextualized and editorialized. A data point might be valuable to you: "Joe Smith won the election to the school board." It won't mean much to people who don't know who Joe Smith is or how his particular policies will impact the community.

The good news is, you can combine a wealth of digital sources of information and knowledge, editorial and context, and configure them to be automatically delivered to you whenever you're online.

DIGITAL DICTIONARY

RSS (really simple syndication):

A tool used by online publications that groups all their articles into one easy-to-read "feed," or chronological list. Avid online readers use RSS to group all of their favorite online publishers in one place, which can be consumed in many different ways, including on their Google homepage, in Microsoft Outlook and on a smartphone. Online readers tend to consume from a large selection of varied sources, which if read in full would be haltingly cumbersome. RSS features an easy-to-skim "title and heading"-style display, allowing readers to pick and choose which articles they want to skip and which to spend time with.

Get Google Smart

To stay relevant in the information age, you must master Google. It should be as comfortable as breathing. Google can deliver on all the aforementioned currencies of the web, but it is the king of intention. That is its primary purpose. It seeks to discover your intention and, based on that, deliver the most relevant information it can. While most websites are desperate to retain visitors, Google boasts about how quickly users leave their page. Google's ultimate goal is to have a user type in a search, immediately find an appropriate link, follow that link within two seconds and not return.

So, how does one master Google? I could spend the next 50 pages outlining strategies and tactics, share favorite online information hotspots and generally bore you to death with buckets and buckets of fish you can't possibly eat in one sitting. Instead, I'm going to teach you to fish.

By this point, you've almost certainly made a few thousand searches on Google. You probably enter a couple of keywords and hit Search. Often, that will get a satisfactory result. But satisfactory is so rarely satisfying. Go to a computer and head to Google. Right now, out there on the web, is a far more comprehensive and current list of tactics for getting the most out of Google than I could ever put in this book. Let's call them cheats. So type in "Google cheats" (no quotes). You'll probably get a mix of strange results: maybe a YouTube video or two, cheat codes for a video game you've never heard of and some strange directory webpage full of ads that's almost certainly a scam. Not the information superhighway we were hoping for. Now, go back to the Google homepage and type the same thing slowly, one word at a time, and don't hit Search right away. You'll notice Google has helpfully listed a number of popular search terms that flesh out our original search of Google cheats. Because of their insanely advanced algorithm and trillions of historical searches, Google has become very, very good at understanding what you're looking for. It's very likely that Google will offer a suggestion near the top of that list called "Google cheat sheet." Click on that suggestion. The very first result will almost certainly be Google's own cheat sheet for making your searches more effective, and just about all of the results on the first page will be useful to you. Explore them, and you will discover how to do many wondrous things with Google, like these:

- Search for exact phrase matches

- Search for all websites that link to a particular domain

- Search within a domain

- Search for only results that were published within the last 30 days

- Search for this term but exclude results including that term

- Search for only copyright-free material

These and many other Google tactics will dramatically increase your efficiency and effectiveness while you search. As with all things digital, the best way of learning is by doing. Experiment and play on a daily basis, and you'll soon find yourself increasingly comfortable manhandling Google.

SEO High

As you might imagine, websites that appear in the first page of a search result are extremely valuable. They get the most clicks, are considered more authoritative sources of information and are generally seen as the hot real estate of the web. If you're trying to sell bathtub moonshine, you want your website to be the first result on a search for "bathtub moonshine." The process of massaging this system is called search engine optimization, or SEO for short. This is an extremely technical and wonky topic full of specialists who make boatloads of money in consultancy fees. It's a rapidly changing paradigm that Google tweaks all the time, so the best practices change constantly. For updated resources on SEO, visit www.OvercomingTheDigitalDivide.com.

However, there are a few key anchor ideas, which will remain a staple of SEO that everyone should be aware of. The first are keywords. In our moonshiner example, the words "bathtub" and "moonshine" are keywords. Using these keywords in a domain hostname and in the title of a page and using the term often within the body of a page increases the density (frequency of occurrence) of the keyword. Google likes this. Google also likes frequently updated content. One of the reasons blogs have become so popular is that their frequent updates keep the attention of Google, forcing it to continually pay attention to the blog. Blogs also trade a lot of links back and forth, and to be honest, Google treats the web like a high school clique: you better know somebody to be somebody. The more inbound links, or links from other websites that lead to yours, the better. Additionally, the more important Google considers the source of the inbound link, the more weight it gives it.

For a quick understanding of how important Google considers a URL, look at its Pagerank. Pagerank is a ranged system valued 1 through 10 representing the top-level effectiveness of a site's SEO. Using our high school clique analogy, a Pagerank of 1 would represent the antisocial dork playing Dungeons and Dragons in his basement. A Pagerank of 10 would be the overachieving homecoming queen who just got a full ride to Harvard. You know which one you'd rather be. If you're curious about Pagerank, I recommend you download the Google Toolbar. The Google Toolbar is a useful add-on to your web browser that offers lots of web surfing enhancements, notably an overview of a webpage's Pagerank. You can download it at toolbar.google.com. After installing the toolbar, it will appear in your web browser, just below the address bar. You'll notice a section in the middle titled Pagerank, with a horizontal green bar next to it (if it does not automatically appear, just right click on the toolbar and add it). That bar is a visual approximation of a site's Pagerank, and holding your cursor over that bar will display a site's exact Pagerank. This is a great way to quickly and easily figure out how important a site is to Google.

Although most people think that Pagerank is named for its function of ranking webpages, it is actually named for Google cofounder Larry Page.

Why Google Is Unique

Before we move on from this section, it's worth considering the monumental power of Google. Never before in history has a single media entity been both a medium and a metric. Google is not only the way we *get* our information, but the way we *judge* our information. You use Google to find something, then judge the authority of that something based on how Google shows it to you. This effect is so powerful that nearly 90% of all clicks from a search happen on the first page of results. Adding in the second page, this number jumps to nearly 100%.[8]

This is an incredible amount of power.

Add to this the fact that tools like Google Analytics and Google AdSense dramatically affect the decision-making process of most of the businesses in the United States, and Google starts to look a little scary. Microsoft's infamous antimonopoly scandal for bundling a silly little web browser with their operating system seems laughably unimportant in comparison.

That said, nobody need panic. Seemingly aware of this lopsided power structure, the company has adopted "Don't Be Evil" as its unofficial motto.[9] In any event, most of what Google does is pretty transparent, and when it isn't, Google is acutely aware that they are being watched very, very carefully. A veritable army of geeks tweak and tamper with the search process continually to see what works and what doesn't. Many of these factors are outside of Google's control, like how many inbound links a page has, how respected the sites sending those inbound links are, how well matched the text on the page is to the search term, where the page links out to, and so on. Some have argued that search is a public good, that we should use an open source, publicly controlled search algorithm. That argument is foolish. Any such system would be far more prone to malevolent tampering than

---

[8]http://electronplumber.com/number-of-clicks-for-ranking-first-in-google-vs-all-the-rest/
[9]http://investor.google.com/conduct.html

anything Google would try to pull. Besides, while it's the undisputed champion, Google is not the only game in town. The management at Bing, Yahoo and Ask would salivate at the opportunity to capitalize on a breach of public trust from Google.

Google is an exceptionally innovative company and enjoys one of the few American executive teams that seem to seek long-term vision over quarterly profit growth. This is nothing to bemoan; it's something to celebrate. Let's hope Google continues to exemplify its "Don't Be Evil" motto.

DIGITAL DICTIONARY

Open source:

Generally, refers to software whose source code is publicly available. Open source software permits its users to study, modify and improve upon it, often resulting in collaborative, group-developed software. WordPress and Linux are extremely popular examples of open source software.

Chapter 6: Social Networks

Why Social Networks Are Important

As we briefly reviewed in Chapter 3, social networks are a critical and required component of success in digital life. They truly represent a paradigm shift in the way human beings engage with the world around them. It sounds grandiose, but it's true.

A well-crafted social network "pushes" information, creating an ambient awareness of the world around you. Instead of dogmatically seeking out information, news and entertainment, your friends, colleagues and industry peers will personally recommend them for you. Some believe this interconnection and personalization will allow social networks (specifically, Facebook) to usurp Google as the primary source of information organization on the web. Think about it. How would you prefer to find a new sushi restaurant? By thumbing through an itemized directory, by reading the detached reviews of professional critics, or through the recommendation of a trusted friend? Fred Vogelstein, whose feature in *Wired Magazine* was both prescient and wildly entertaining, sums up the epic battle to organize the web:

> For the last decade or so, the Web has been defined by Google's algorithms—rigorous and efficient equations that parse practically every byte of online activity to build a dispassionate atlas of the online world. Facebook CEO Mark Zuckerberg envisions a more personalized, humanized Web, where our network of friends, colleagues, peers, and family is our primary source of information, just as it is offline. In Zuckerberg's vision, users will query this "social graph" to find a doctor, the best camera, or someone to hire—rather than tapping the cold mathematics of a Google search.[10]

A full reading of Fred's excellent editorial is highly recommended.

---

[10]http://www.wired.com/techbiz/it/magazine/17-07/ff_facebookwall

Social networks don't just allow you to receive information, but convey it as well. It is difficult to describe how useful this can be. The rewards need to be experienced to be fully appreciated, as individual networks provide benefits unique to your social circle. In a more general sense, conveying something through your social network is a low-density, high-volume opportunity to engage in a more meaningful way. A quick status update, a posted link, a tagged photo, an uploaded video – all are easy, quick invitations to further exploration. Far less demanding than a phone call or email, interactions on your social network are at leisure and apropos by self-selection. An effective social network can help you find a dining companion when traveling, troubleshoot a computing error, sniff out better vendor rates, hire a new salesperson, sell unwanted office supplies, share your grandmother's famous baklava recipe or find an nth degree connection to the prime minister of Malaysia – anything and everything. It's up to you to cultivate a network germane to your needs while maintaining a presence that supports them.

Beyond the hyperintimate utility of it, social networking is the catalyst of all things viral. It is the kingmaker of singing hamsters, dancing wedding parties and doped-up postsurgical nine-year-olds everywhere. But low-culture fluff is just the tip of the social iceberg. Beneath the surface lie veritable worlds of insider information and in-vertical indispensables. Increasingly, this is becoming big business (the ad agency/CORPCOM/PR land grab on viral and social media marketing budget helps). The year 2009 was the first time in history that major media outlets received more traffic to their web platforms from Facebook than from Google. It is a trend that will only continue and quite possibly the shape of things to come.

Remember Fred's article? Really, read it.

Getting Started

If I haven't sufficiently convinced you by this point to *use* social networks, at the very least take my advice on this: stake your territory. Many social networks have profiles that are uniquely labeled, and once that moniker is claimed, no one else can use it. Apologies to the John and Jane Smiths of the world, but while you still can, create profiles and claim your name in as ideal a form as possible on Twitter, Facebook and LinkedIn. On Twitter, this process is automatic – any profile name you choose is unique. On Facebook, it is as simple as creating an account, then visiting http://www.facebook.com/username/ to claim your vanity

URL. On LinkedIn, you must create a profile, then while logged in click Edit My Profile. In the top block description, you'll find a listing called Public Profile followed by your current URL identity. Click Edit to the right of that URL and select an available, unique URL for your profile.

But what good is a simple, easy-to-find and easy-to-share social web profile if you don't use it? We reviewed the largest social networking communities and their respective cultures briefly in Chapter 3. By no means is that an exhaustive list. There are dozens of sizeable social networks, each with its own distinct personality and specialization. Photographers can display their work on the world stage with Flickr. Generation Y (and those looking for their perspective and talents) can find tremendous resources and a robust community on Brazen Careerist. A presence on Yelp is practically a necessity for anyone operating a local business. There are social networks for scientific researchers, film buffs, global travelers and almost everything in between. It is up to you to decide if participation in a niche network is appropriate and worthwhile. This list is a good jumping-off point for research into various social networks: http://en.wikipedia. org/wiki/List_of_social_networking_websites.

Regardless of niche participation, every working professional should cover the bases on the two, arguably three, nexus networks. Facebook and LinkedIn are nonnegotiable parts of digital life. Too big and too important to ignore, they represent the global online general (Facebook) and business (LinkedIn) communities. Twitter has cemented itself in the public consciousness and is a "Who's Who" gathering for anyone even tangentially involved with politics, tech or media. This is quickly growing to incorporate more and more people every day and is an *excellent* place to listen to conversations about things that are important to you.

As you incorporate social networking into your daily life, you'll revitalize old connections, discover new ones and generally enjoy the benefits of socializing in the digital age. But at all times, participate with purpose. Do you want an extremely tight-knit, reliable LinkedIn network? Then don't accept and invite casual professional connections, just those whom you work closely with. How personal will you be on Facebook? If it's all about coordinating ski weekends and reconnecting with old friends, consider keeping professional contacts outside your network or limiting their access to your profile using Facebook's privacy settings. If you want to use Twitter as a personal branding tool, then follow only those relevant to your industry, foster relationships with those you respect and always tweet on message. In almost all cases, quality trumps quantity. The lure of amassing followers like baseball cards and the naiveté of accepting every friend request can be powerful. This network needs to work for you. Follow those whom *you* find useful, friend those whom *you* like and curate the network to support *your* goals.

Just always be mindful of each network's culture and unspoken etiquette. Some are obvious: don't upload embarrassing photos of your friends. Some are less so: be consistent in the frequency of your tweets. As you use each network more and more, you will organically glean what is and is not acceptable, but a Google search for "etiquette" and the network in question is a good jumping-off point.

Power Tips

No words will be wasted on step-by-steps of how to set up or accomplish specific tasks within each network. It's mostly intuitive, and any trouble is easily overcome through Google or the network's help section. The actual doing of social networking changes too often to put to print. *Much* more useful and interesting are the out-of-the-box ways the networks can be used. The possibilities are probably endless, but here are a few ideas to get you thinking in the right direction.

Share, Track and Learn

One of the most rewarding, easy and fun things to do on social networks is posting links to content your network will find valuable. It's a fantastic way to help your contacts find relevant needles in the giant, nebulous haystack of the web. Share breaking news and thoughtful commentary, highlight what you find inspirational, useful or entertaining and use it as a platform to promote your own work. Unfortunately, the URLs you want to share can get very long and confusing. They are hard to remember, often break in emails and don't fit on networks (like Twitter) that impose a character limit on updates. As a solution to this problem, many web services have sprung up called URL Shorteners. They take a convoluted URL and change it into something short and sweet. There are a lot of options on this front, many with a unique little bell or whistle. Bit.ly – is a popular URL[11] shortening utility, offering robust metrics of who, where and what clicks you are generating. Since understanding your audience and their intention is a digital currency, it should go without saying that this information is valuable. Bit.ly identifies which of your links are most popular, what days and times result in the most clicks, what network clicks are being generated on, where in the world your audience is clicking from, who else shared the same link you did and other

[11]http://bit.ly/

actionable insights. As you use Bit.ly to shorten and share links, it automatically tracks these data. Use this information to your advantage.

> Netiquette is more than a cute play on the word "etiquette." Each social network has a culture. Spend a few minutes to learn the dos and don'ts.

Pre-Networking

You will soon discover one of online networking's best attributes is its ability to efficiently organize offline networking. Whether it's an invitation on Facebook or a regular gathering on Meetup.com, coordinating events with social networks is an easy, helpful tool for event managers of every stripe. And the public RSVP can be made extremely useful to you. After agreeing to attend a networking event, find the other attendees on the event page. From here you can find out exactly who will be joining you at the event. Explore who they are and what they do. Identify the individuals you want to meet; find common interests, icebreakers and potential points of partnership. This information coupled with their profile pictures will uniquely equip you to work the room with a seemingly magic touch!

Prospecting

Social networks are goldmines of potential new clients, customers, partners and employees; you only need know how to look. Certainly, forming fresh connections through organic interaction and polling your existing network are great ways to search for prospective stakeholders, but sometimes a more active approach is required. For this, LinkedIn is a godsend. The site's Advanced Search function (next to the search box on the top navigation bar) is incredibly powerful. You can filter your search results by job title, company, industry, geography, language and degree of connection to you. In practice, this means you can discover current marketing directors at any given company, account reps who used to work in the automotive vertical or highly recommended consultants based in your area. Your search will yield only results that are within three degrees of connection (i.e., a connection of a connection of your connection) or a fellow member of a LinkedIn group you participate in – just one more reason to maintain a robust LinkedIn presence.

It is also important to note that LinkedIn is a commercial service, and it is doing its best to charge for services it believes you will pay for. Should you? If you are actively looking for work or if you are constantly looking for connections and prospective clients, the paid functions of LinkedIn may be a very good investment.

Twitter Apps

Truth be told, Twitter as a standalone web property sucks. It's hard to follow conversations back and forth, difficult to browse and prune your followers and not always clear on how to discover new, interesting people to follow. The strength of Twitter (and most of the web's hottest properties) is its API. Using this API, scores of developers create applications, widgets and websites, all dedicated to making Twitter better.

Using these third-party Twitter applications and services, you can do the following:

- Organize and filter your Twitter feed for keywords and specific users
- Schedule your tweets for delayed posting
- Auto-respond to new followers by following back, messaging and/or replying to them
- Search directories of influential Twitter users
- Explore deeper into trending topics
- Track keywords within the "Twitterverse"
- Manage multiple Twitter accounts
- Compare your Twitter reach and activity to others
- See who of those you follow are following you back
- Stop following inactive users
- Integrate your blog's RSS
- Geotag your tweets

There are literally hundreds of applications and add-ons available, and they

DIGITAL DICTIONARY

API (application programming interface):

The part of a software program that allows the program to interact with other software. On the web, APIs are commonly made publicly available by proprietary developers in the hope of enabling and inspiring third-party development of supplemental software.

DIGITAL DICTIONARY

Geotag:

To add geographically relevant data to various forms of media. In practice, this often results in latitudinal and longitudinal coordinates being stored within everything from photographs to Twitter updates.

are truly what make Twitter great. You'll need to discover which tools are most useful to you on your own. As you get started, I recommend using WeFollow (www.wefollow.com) to discover the most influential users on a given topic and TweetCloud (www.tweetcloud.com) to explore the network around a particular topic or user more deeply. Once you've found a few people to follow, try using Trendistic (www.trendistic.com) to learn more about trending topics and how certain conversations "grow" on Twitter. After you've been tweeting a while, you may find it necessary to prune or otherwise moderate whom you follow versus who follows you; use Friend or Follow (www.friendorfollow.com) for that.

The more you use Twitter, the more you'll understand what's uniquely useful to you. Identify those needs and Google around for a solution; it's probably out there.

LinkedIn Optimization

The assumption here is that you already have a complete, up-to-date LinkedIn profile. If any of the basics are missing, like employment history, a professional photograph or education, stop reading and complete your profile now. Once the fundamentals are covered, consider investing time into optimizing your presence on LinkedIn. First and foremost, utilize your profile as a search hub. With a network Pagerank of 9, LinkedIn carries a great deal of "Google juice." In other words, it appears often in search results and is a great source to link out of. Craft your profile with SEO in mind, using keywords appropriate to your area of expertise often. Make use of the Websites section of your profile, but don't use the generic My Company or My Blog headings. Instead, select Other when editing that section of your profile and optimize the outbound link's title with something more descriptive. LinkedIn calls the byline directly underneath your name a "professional heading" and automatically labels it with your current job title. It might be a good idea to edit that heading to something with a little more pop, like your personal brand. After all, the heading appears in search results and is often the first thing people see; use it as an opportunity to stand out from the crowd.

And while LinkedIn is certainly one of the more static social networks out there, there are some unique areas for participation that other networks do not offer. One useful area is the Answers function, in which users pose and respond to questions within different areas of expertise. This is a fantastic way to learn from others and attract visibility on the network. As a bonus, if one of your responses is selected as the best answer by the user who posed the question, you get an "expertise point," which is displayed on your profile. You should also join and contribute to groups relevant to your industry. Members of the group have increased direct access to each other and provide a platform to discuss issues of mutual interest, share news and fill jobs.

Finally, request and write recommendations to trusted colleagues and clients. A highly recommended professional profile engenders trust among new connections and archives a positive remembrance in the minds of those who recommend you. Just be careful to only request recommendations from those you truly know and trust. In the same way you'd personally check with someone before listing them as a reference, check to see if a recommendation request is welcome and would benefit you.

Use Photos

People are visual creatures. Photos attract interest and engage people in a way text simply cannot, particularly in the crowded, hurried halls of social networks. This is especially true on Facebook, where viewing others' photographs is one of the most common and popular activities. In practice, this means photos should be used on Facebook whenever possible to draw attention. When sharing a link, select a photo thumbnail to go alongside the post. That post is much more likely to be clicked on than the link alone. As you go about your daily life, take pictures with your smartphone of the moments and memories you'd like to share, then upload them on the go, along with a contextual caption. Snapshots of that amusing bit of "public art" you came across, the brilliantly presented main course at a newly discovered restaurant or the delay and cancellation ticker as you kill time at the airport – all are great ways to connect with your social network. You may be surprised how useful and entertaining this kind of mobile "photocasting" can be. Furthermore, when using photos on Facebook, be sure to use the tag feature. Tagging someone simply means assigning a named caption to someone depicted in a photograph. If they are one of your Facebook friends, the caption will automatically link to their profile and the photo will appear in your friend's newsfeed. In a professional setting, this can be a phenomenal way to stay connected after an offline event and increase visibility among your friends' friends. One cautionary note: Asking permission to tag your friends in a picture you post is becoming more and more commonplace. Some people insist upon it. Which begs for the question: If you have friends in your network that you need to "ask before you tag," should they be in your network?

Save Time

Managing multiple social profiles can be a cumbersome, time-consuming task, especially if you're more or less posting the same content over and over to each network. Ping.fm[12] is one solution (there are many others). Ping.fm is an online service that allows you to post to many different social media profiles with a single update. With support for dozens of different social networks, this is a must-have time saver for social media power users. For a list of other third-party tools that help streamline your social media activity, check www.OvercomingTheDigitalDivide. com.

Stay Current

The tips listed here are *far* from comprehensive. The creative, unique and powerful ways social networks can be leveraged for your professional benefit are nearly endless. And with each network continually changing its interface and features, wholly new opportunities will develop over time. Make it a point to seek out articles and blogs that offer tips on how to utilize social networks to your professional benefit, and you'll always stay one step ahead of the curve.

The 1% Rule

When you participate in online communities, it's worth understanding a phenomenon that emerged as part of the Web 2.0 movement called the 1% rule, or the 1-9-90 rule. The idea is pretty simple: in any user-generated environment, 90% of users are viewers only, contributing no content; 9% of users are infrequent contributors or "editors" who interact with existing content and 1% of users are heavy contributors, creating the bulk of new content. The principle holds up surprisingly well across a vast spectrum of web communities that rely on user participation.

DIGITAL DICTIONARY

Web 2.0:

Often used to describe the perception of a generational shift in web development and web design. However, it was actually the name of an O'Reilly trade conference that occurred when the shift from rich data websites to rich media websites began.

What does this have to do with you? Two things: (1) On any network you manage, be it your e-commerce cart, personal blog or Facebook profile, make it as easy as possible for your audience to participate. Remove unnecessary barriers of entry, provide multiple paths of participation

[12]http://www.ping.fm/

and actively invite contributions. Over time, the 1% of your audience/users will become known to you. Embrace these evangelists with gusto. Identify them, applaud them, foster personal relationships, offer them special benefits and otherwise do everything in your power to keep them on your side. They are your closest digital allies and the most powerful marketing tool you have. And (2) if you want to speed your way to a larger digital presence, become one of the 1% who truly interact with and help create the web. You will be surprised by how fast your digital star will rise.

The Fallacy of Privacy

Much has been said, bemoaned really, about the death of privacy in the digital age. Social networks are at the front and center of this shift, but every text message, email, paperless bill, GPS-guided trip, website visit and credit card purchase tells an incredibly complete tale. Your extremely personal tale, with very little hidden. Ignored perhaps, but not hidden. Most of us think that we are safe because we are, for all practical purposes, anonymous. So what if you call home from the bowling alley and tell the wife you're at choir practice? She won't know, and no one will care. True enough. As a practical matter, it is very unlikely that a tabloid television show or magazine would care to use this bit of information in any way. But her lawyer will make extraordinary use of it during your divorce negotiations. How that lawyer will obtain this information is child's play.

The meteoric fall from grace Tiger Woods suffered is instructive here. It's the 21st- century, and in our time, there is absolutely no reasonable expectation of privacy. Not for philandering politicians, or megastar athletes, or for you or me. This lesson should not be lost on anyone. Few are as famous as Tiger, but when a significant other, prospective employer or IRS investigator wants to catch you doing something you shouldn't be doing, they will use the same tools to incriminate you: your browser history, your text message stack, your mobile phone records, the MAC addresses

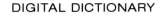

DIGITAL DICTIONARY

MAC address (media access control address):

A unique, alphanumeric code used to identify a piece of Internet-connected hardware.

of your electronic devices, your electronic credit card receipts, the GPS chip in your phone, any Facebook quiz you ever took, Google Earth, Google Latitude and Google History. There are so many places you leave an electronic trail, so obviously yours, even an unmotivated semi-tech-savvy 14-year-old could trap you. Your life is an open e-book. Mine too. And that's the point.

So, here are the guidelines for living your digital life in the 21st- century. Do not type or text anything you do not wish to make part of the permanent body of knowledge of mankind. You can't take it back, ever. Remember that every voicemail you leave is a digital recording. Don't take pictures you don't want your mother to see. And lastly, do not ever think that an electronic transaction is private. It may be secure, but a secure transaction is not a private one. Someone, somewhere, has complete (as in absolute, total, full) access to your financial data when you make an electronic transaction. They may not be in a position to hurt you in any way, but when someone wants to know if a transaction took place, there is no such thing as an anonymous electronic transaction. Ask former New York State Governor Eliot Spitzer.

Of special note here are social networks, particularly Facebook. If you drill down to the Privacy Settings area from the Settings link on your Facebook profile, you will be presented with a simplified list of options. If you have not already done so, take a minute right now, open a browser and follow along. Go to Facebook, click Account, and then select Privacy Settings from the drop-down menu. You can make a universal decision on how your information is shared (i.e., everyone, friends of friends or friends only), or by selecting Custom you can decide one by one what type of information can be seen by whom. Click Edit Your Settings under the Applications and Websites section at the bottom of the privacy page, and select what type of information you want to make available to third-party application developers and websites that work with Facebook.

I acknowledge there is value in the modicum of privacy that these controls afford, but much of that privacy remains an illusion. The real danger to your privacy is not from your friends or friends of friends (though absolutely nothing is stopping them from sharing your "private" updates in a more public forum), it's from Facebook itself.

Facebook is described in many different ways. To some, it is a community. Others call it a social network. Still others say it is a conversation. Fair descriptions, but all wrong. Facebook is a commercial enterprise based in Silicon Valley. It is a for-profit venture with the goal of increasing shareholder value. No decision is made about the community on Facebook without a group of very serious, profit-minded executives thinking through how the decision will impact the bottom line, the cap chart, the exit strategy, and so on.

For most people, this is not an issue. If fame, access and better communication are your goals, Facebook delivers. However, Facebook privacy is an illusion at best. If you want your information to be truly private, it doesn't make sense to publish it to a community of hundreds of millions of users, and it never will.

None of this is being said to scare you. Truthfully, we crossed this bridge a long time ago with credit cards, cell towers and closed-circuit television. No one is suggesting you retrograde to an analog-only hermit. Our open digital kimonos spur wonderful new technologies that make the world a better place to live. It is simply something to acknowledge, and a poignant reminder: if you wouldn't want it in the newspaper, don't make it digital.

Chapter 7:
Information Management

"I don't know" is no longer an acceptable answer to anything. Facts, news and relationships are no longer limited by access, but by information management. Whether you realize it or not, any gap in your knowledge is caused solely by information overload. Or, as Clay Shirky, the famous Internet technologies thinker and author of *Here Comes Everybody: The Power of Organizing Without Organizations*, puts it, "filter failure." By now you should understand the critical roles Google and social networks play in managing the incredible breadth and depth of data in our lives and on the web. Powerful as they may be, they are not enough. Establishing personalized, automated processes to cope with this deluge of information is the only way to thrive in the digital age.

Contacts

You may not think of them this way, but your relationships are data points in your life. Whom you know, how you know them, what they do and what you have planned with them are incredibly detailed pieces of information. Organizing and optimizing these critical data points is a favor you do for everyone involved.

Here's an example. At some time in your life, you have wanted to spread the word about something to a group of people. Did you fire up an email client, add a bunch of addresses to the BCC line and send that "Hey All" message to yourself? Even worse, did you just add email addresses on the Send or CC line, broadcasting the personal contact information of your connections to each other?

You totally blew that opportunity.

That email looked just like spam. It read like spam. It felt like spam. Honestly, it was spam. Now, your contacts probably didn't try to get your email address blacklisted, but they probably didn't give your missive much attention, either. Computers are incredibly good at organizing and automating repetitive functions. Using tools created for customer relationship management (CRM), you can effectively turn Brand You into a powerhouse of connection.

Inexpensive, in-the-cloud software like Mailchimp (http://www.mailchimp.com) can create template emails with personalized salutations and individual customization that look, smell and taste like you sat down and wrote a single message. As you add contacts to your database, another simple-to-use, in-the-cloud software, Highrise (http://highrisehq.com/), can include notes about them, allowing you to keep track of important personal details and prompt a more high-touch exchange with your network. One of the most important features in this software (and any true contact management or consumer relationship marketing program) is the ability to set up tickler files for each of your contacts. In this context, a tickler file is a simple, time-sensitive prompt to reconnect with important but more occasional connections. Remind yourself to congratulate a former colleague about his receiving his MBA. Don't forget to reach out to the recruiter you met in the airport a few months ago. Or simply stay on top of the regular check-ins with friends, family and associates we all mean to make time for but who always seem to get lost in the shuffle. For a list of contact management resources, visit www.OvercomingTheDigitalDivide.com.

You will be *shocked* at how much mental bandwidth a system of notes, tasks and ticklers frees up and the peace of mind it bestows. Much of this can even be accomplished using the notes, tasks and calendar functions in programs like Apple Mail and Microsoft Office, but a relatively small investment in dedicated CRM software really makes a big difference. You will be grateful for the dividends it yields.

A final word on contact management: it's up to you to follow through. How many times have you attended a networking event, gathered a smattering of business cards, tossed them onto the pile in your desk the next day and promptly forgotten about them? You may as well have thrown them away. Worthwhile networks aren't built by rubbing elbows; they're built with elbow grease. The day after meeting new contacts, add their information to your contact management system, including any personal tidbit you gleaned in the notes section and a tickler reminder to follow up as appropriate. Always draft a brief email note, letting them know you enjoyed meeting them and

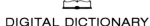

DIGITAL DICTIONARY

Cloud computing:

Internet-based computing, in which information, resources and software are supplied to the user online, rather than through installed programs.

look forward to following up on future opportunities. Set up a tickler to follow up in a month, or put them on whatever schedule makes sense for you. Depending on your social network strategy, you may wish to add them as connections on your Facebook, Twitter and LinkedIn accounts. This small bit of extra effort is the difference between an incoherent, unreliable set of contacts and a priceless, tightly knit network.

Information

There are tens of billions of indexed pages on the web right now. Those pages change all the time, and the raw number gets bigger every single day. The content creation cascade that started with Gutenberg and his printing press has arrived at an unfathomably huge portion and pace. No human being could ever process even a fraction of this body of knowledge. Your only hope is to identify what's important and make machines curate the mess for you.

This concept is called a Listening Post, and there are a host of digital tools to help you. But tools are just tools. It's up to you to use them intelligently. Identifying relevant topics, verticals, authors and news sources is a task uniquely suited to and achievable by you and you alone.

RSS Readers

We defined RSS briefly in Chapter 5. As a reminder, they are simple feeds of content which users can conveniently consume in software called "readers." There are a lot of RSS readers out there. Google

RSS Icon

Reader is a great one, and I highly recommend it. It is accessible from any web-connected device, can share articles with others, can save items to an archive and much more. Ultimately, the choice of reader is up to you. More important is the process of choosing and organizing a reasonably consumable number of feeds you will view on a daily basis. While browsing any blog or news site, you're almost certain to find an RSS icon, often within the address bar on the right side, but somewhere on the site at the very least. Clicking that icon will bring up the RSS feed page. Copy that page's URL and paste it to your reader to begin receiving a continual digest of the site's content in your reader. Almost any RSS reader will allow you to create folders or sections which can house multiple RSS feeds. By taking a little time to organize your feeds into different folders, you can consume topical areas of interest in customized sections. Get as granular (The Red Sox) or as broad (Sports) as you like with these, whatever you find most valuable. Some RSS feeds will display full entries, while others will display only the title and first few lines of the article. Either way, use your RSS reader to skim a daily digest that's important to you, and click through on content that deserves more specific attention. And don't forget: RSS feeds are available for all kinds of content you might not expect, like YouTube channels, Flickr user uploads, Twitter feeds and Wikipedia articles.

Google Alerts

Vigilance in the digital age is exhausting. A single person might need to keep tabs on competitors, watch for any personal press mentions, monitor specific brand references and be in the know about a developing story. Manually tracking all this would be a wasteful, thankless task. Google is (once again) to the rescue. Using its Alerts tool (www.google.com/alerts), you can automate any Google search for instantaneous, daily or weekly monitoring. This includes any customized or "hacked" search you discovered in Chapter 5. The Google Alert system will automatically send an email at the frequency you select summarizing any new Google results for the entered search terms. Alternatively, you can have Google send these alerts via an RSS feed. You can submit up to 1,000 different alerts, so use this incredible tool to your advantage to stay at the cutting edge on all sorts of business and personal intelligence. Like most of the services from Google, it's completely free, quick to set up and easy to use.

Social Bookmarking

You likely come across some useful post, article, list, case study, reference material, resource or tip every day. It's a big part of what makes the web such a rewarding place. How do you keep track of all these myriad pieces of content? It had better not be your browser's bookmarking feature. Those bookmarks are difficult to organize, hard to browse at any sizeable volume and locked to the specific browser and computer they're on.

Enter social bookmarking, a web-based method of referencing, organizing, searching and sharing what used to be stuck in a local web browser. Social bookmarks offer three key advantages over traditional browser-based bookmarks. First, since they are stored online, your bookmarks are available anytime you're on the web. Keep the same bookmarks on your home desktop, laptop, work desktop and coffee shop kiosk. Second, they can store metadata in each bookmark. This metadata (generally tags and notes) are fully searchable and a great way of organizing huge volumes of bookmarks. Finally, social bookmarks are easily sharable. New bookmarks can immediately be sent to email addresses and social media profiles. Even better, much in the same vein as social networks, social bookmarking sites allow you to subscribe to other users' bookmarks and create groups of contacts that automatically share bookmarks with each other.

There are a few of these services out there, but Delicious is strongly recommended. Delicious is a popular, easy-to-use and feature-full social bookmarking service on the web. It offers a downloadable add-on which will integrate itself into your web browser, offering increased access to and one-click additions of your social bookmarks.

DIGITAL DICTIONARY

Metadata:

Data that describe other data. More generally, metadata are additional information stored within various forms of media and electronic files such as photographs, videos, documents, websites and database entries. Metadata encompass all kinds of information like keywords, date/ time stamping, author identity and geographic info.

Discovery

We have only been discussing how to manage and organize data that are apparent, namely, whom you know, what you like and what you need to remember. But what was known yesterday won't suffice tomorrow. The web is a phenomenal place of discovery. Using a few digital techniques and resources, you'll always have a fresh infusion of thoughts, news and content to keep you at the cutting edge and share with your larger network.

Crowdsourcing

Crowdsourcing is an important concept that plays a key role in digital discovery. The term was coined by Jeff Howe in his June 2006[13] feature in *Wired Magazine*. It's a conflation of the words "crowd" and "outsourcing," referring to the assignment of tasks typically fulfilled by outside contractors to a large group of people who compete or cooperate to complete the task. The idea is to harness the economy and wisdom of crowds to achieve results unavailable from a traditional, single-source service. If two heads are better than one, two thousand heads are a whole lot better. Enabled by the collaborative nature of the web, crowdsourcing services have blossomed as a legitimate implementation option for a stunning variety of tasks:

- Kluster (www.kluster.com) is a brainstorming and feedback network offering "a new breed of group decision-making tool that helps you bubble-

[13]http://www.wired.com/wired/archive/14.06/crowds.html

up new ideas, identify the best ones, and make better decisions."

- 99Designs (www.99designs.com) offers conceptualization and creation of graphic design tasks, major and minor.

- uTest (www.utest.com) has 20,000 quality assurance professionals who can help check the user experience of any website or application before it goes to mass market.

- Amazon's Mechanical Turk (www.mturk.com) is a scalable workforce for what they've dubbed Human Intelligence Tasks, or more simply, an assignment that needs an actual brain, but probably not an advanced degree, to complete.

Many more of these services, offering everything from data cleansing and entry to help coming up with product and brand names, are scattered throughout the web. If you need extra brainpower, or simply an inexpensive, efficient means of outsourcing digital labor, crowdsourcing is a fantastic resource.

Reddit

What if the role of a news editor was filled not by a single person, but by the collective hive-mind of news consumers? Reddit is a social news source and online community in which users submit stories to categories of interest after which members of the community then "upvote" the stories they approve of. The more "upvotes" a story receives, the more likely it is to reach the front page of Reddit, providing *tremendous* visibility. An article on the front page of Reddit receives tens of thousands, if not hundreds of thousands, of viewers. In addition to a general interest section, Reddit offers hundreds of subcategories ranging from business and political news to basketball and movies. Reddit's ability to quickly and accurately pick up big stories and useful content on a daily basis is astounding. It's a major stop on "The Daily Me" for many, many people.

DIGITAL DICTIONARY

"The Daily Me":

A term describing the daily consumption of news personalized toward individual taste, often through automated and algorithmic means. The term originated from Nicholas Negroponte, founder of the MIT Media Lab.

A minor caveat: the Reddit community can be a cloistered group. The top users are rumored to drive much of the site's editorial action (the 1% rule has downsides, too), and the community as a whole tends to fall into a certain demographic: white, educated males aged 18–34 who *really* like technology. Naturally, this skews the results toward a specific worldview, and certain topics (Apple) are more rigorously covered than others (feminism). There is a certain juvenility to the site, so don't expect it to replace the Business section of the *Wall Street Journal*. However, warts and all, Reddit is a wonderful resource of discovery and an illuminating insight into an important demographic that lives digital every day. After all, the *geek* shall inherit the earth.

StumbleUpon

StumbleUpon is to web surfing what television remotes are to channel surfing; it enables quick, flippant scanning of bite-sized content snacks, one after another. Except StumbleUpon is way cooler than some clunky handheld gadget with sticky buttons. After users install the toolbar into a web browser, the service prompts users to identify areas of interest from over 600 topical categories. Then, using the toolbar, users click the Stumble button, which leads to relevant content throughout the web. Any stumbled site can be "liked" or "disliked," and using those data, StumbleUpon learns user preferences and tastes, tweaking its algorithm to display content increasingly likely to be enjoyed by each user. New content is submitted to StumbleUpon by its users every day, building a nearly endless universe of content to discover. Fair warning: "stumbling" through the web is incredibly useful, fun and addicting. You shouldn't try this the day before a major deadline.

Delicious

Hopefully, you've already decided to start using Delicious as a social bookmarking tool to help you organize and share web pages of note. But Delicious can help with content discovery, too. Similarly to Reddit, as users bookmark various sites, those sites are added to sections on the Delicious.com homepage. Explore which resources people are bookmarking right now, explore which have emerged as particularly popular, or explore bookmarks by specific tags. While Delicious is less popular than Reddit and less personalized than StumbleUpon, it offers a unique approach: this is not what users liked and thought others might like as well; this is what users specifically wanted to save for later reference.

Pandora

This one is here just for fun. Pandora is radio in the digital age – an intelligent, self-programmable web radio station with the ability to learn your musical tastes. It functions by using the database generated from the Music Genome Project, an ongoing effort to analyze and categorize all the music ever recorded, capturing the details that make each genre of music and each song unique – melody, harmony, tempo, instrumentation, lyrics, and so on. All told, each song in the Music Genome Project is categorized by close to 400 attributes. Using this mountain of data, Pandora lets users create their own radio stations by adding a few bands or songs they like. Based off these initial inputs, Pandora automatically creates and transmits a playlist, during which users can "like" or "dislike" individual songs. Very quickly Pandora adapts to each user's personal tastes and modifies the station's playlist to fit. You will be astonished at how precisely Pandora identifies music you love, and how much new music it will help you discover. It is one of my favorite digital toys.

Continuing Professional Education

As the saying goes, when you stop learning, you stop living. The web represents a practically limitless opportunity to learn. The tools and techniques listed in this chapter are not exhaustive. They represent best of breed and personal favorites, but the options for contact management, information administration and knowledge discovery are nearly as endless as the web they seek to organize. Find the sources and tools that work for you. What matters is freeing up brain bandwidth; let a computer deal with retaining and acquiring information, leaving you free to do the things computers can't, like creativity, critical thinking and deal making.

Chapter 8: Hardware and Software

Welcome to the guts of digital life. If you'll allow me to stretch that metaphor a bit, you might think of Google savvy as digital life's higher cognitive function, social networking as charisma and fame, and information management as processing and memory. Hardware and software, then, are the innards. They are the cogs within that make all else possible. Without them, the rest of the system stops.

The recommendations, tools and topics in this chapter are the everyday basics needed to keep ahead of the curve. Some of this will likely require extracurricular study on your part. It doesn't matter how you skill up – trial and error, online tutorials, offline courses – what matters is that you invest the time to set yourself apart. There is no substitution herein; these things separate the out-of-touch and incompetent from their replacements. To be clear, this is simply what is needed on a personal level. The advanced needs of a Small Office/Home Office (SoHo) will be covered in the next chapter.

PC vs. Mac

The eternal debate of fanboy geeks everywhere, the cold, hard truth is that the world, particularly the business world, runs on PC. PCs control 90% of the computing market, and those familiar formats – .doc, .xls, .ppt – aren't going away anytime soon. That being said (and we're likely to enrage quite a few people here), Apple makes a better computer. It's why Apple controls 91% of the computing market priced over $1,000.[14] Apple packs more punch, lasts longer, and, as with all things Apple, produces a sleek, intuitive user experience Microsoft can't seem to match. The pure visceral pleasure of using the Mac OS is far superior to that of Windows. For these reasons, budget allowing it, I recommend purchasing an Apple and running special software that allows both types of OS (Mac and Windows) to

[14]http://www.betanews.com/joewilcox/article/Apple-has-91-of-market-for-1000-PCs-says-NPD/1248313624

operate on the machine. This can be achieved with Apple's own utility called Boot Camp, included in OS X v10.5 (Leopard) or newer. Alternatively, Parallels Desktop, a third-party company, offers an inexpensive option to allow any Apple to function with both the Mac and the Windows OS. Using Parallels, a current-model Mac will be the best Windows computer you've ever owned.

That said, if you are a diehard Microsoft devotee or uninterested in dropping the extra cash on a more expensive Apple model, no real repercussions will come of getting a Dell, HP, Gateway or what have you. I just think you're missing out. What matters much more is staying current. Remember Moore's Law? No matter what the machine's brand is, it will wear out. Fast. Replacing a computer every three to four years is a reasonable down-the-middle split between performance and economy. Replacing it sooner than two years in is just showboating. Anything older than five years is a dinosaur; donate, sell or trash it.

One important note: If you are a power user of Windows and Microsoft Office and you use Windows-specific keyboard shortcuts – you simply have to purchase a computer that has a Windows-specific keyboard. No matter how good (or Mac-centric) Microsoft's Office Mac software is, power users of Excel cannot accomplish what they need to accomplish on a MacBook or MacBook Pro keyboard. Which means Windows power users who want laptops must buy Windows laptops.

Desktop vs. Laptop

You probably don't need a desktop computer. Barring deep use of databases, complex math algorithms, engineering software, advanced video editing/animation or cutting-edge video gaming, laptops are more than capable of doing the job at hand. For most people, that means web surfing, basic office applications, minor photo and video manipulation and email. If that sounds like you, a sole laptop may be the right choice as your primary personal computer. Five to ten years ago, owning both a laptop and desktop had real appeal. That paradigm has changed to owning a personal computer and a smartphone. To that end …

Cell Phone

Not to put too fine a point on it, but no serious person of the digital age should own a cellular telephone. It's fine to keep calling them that, but they are really handheld, function-specific computers. And they are *amazing*. Spurred by the success of the BlackBerry, iPhone and Android, the smartphone market is exploding, and for good reason. Smartphones change the way life is experienced. Constant access to the web means always having the answer. GPS chips and Google Maps mean never being lost. Games, music and videos mean never being bored. This should not be a revelation. You should already own a smartphone. If not – and this cannot be expressed strongly enough – go buy one immediately. In many ways they embody the future of digital life.

One of the most common questions of digital life is which cell phone to get. I reviewed this briefly in Chapter 3; intense email needs used to necessitate a BlackBerry, and web surfing and media viewing used to mean an iPhone or Android. Not anymore. Nowadays, you have your pick of extraordinary handheld computers, app phones, smartphones, tablets and hybrids. Of course, the best cell phone in the world is just an overpriced paperweight without a reliable network backing it up. Choosing a network holds pervasive consequences often far more aggravating than choosing which gadget to keep in your pocket. Forget the commercials; every cellular network has both strong and weak coverage areas. If possible, test different networks in the areas most frequented: your home, office and hangouts. Talk to colleagues in areas you travel in most often and see what their experience has been. Try to select the network that has the strongest, most dependable signal in the areas that matter most to you.

Before we move on, another word on the iPhone/iPod Touch is warranted. Should you decide not to use a smartphone as your primary phone, pick up an iPod Touch or an iPad. They function just like an iPhone, minus the ability to make calls. Notably, they allow access to Apple's app store. I extolled the virtues of the app store in Chapter 3, but they bear repeating. The app store quietly and quickly became *the* reason to own an iPhone, iPod Touch or iPad. Yes, the interface is incredibly fun, slick and sexy, and yes, the quality of its web browsing experience is unmatched. But the app store is the game changer. So much so, it led *New York Times* technology columnist David Pogue to search for a new moniker, finding "smartphone" an outdated term. His result? App phones. To anyone who has used a mobile with an application market, this makes complete sense; apps are the paradigm changer. This is hard to objectively describe. It needs to be emotionalized. You need to peruse the global, digital bazaar that pits established professional developers against a 14-year-old Ukrainian kid with a knack for coding. You need to take in the ocean of apps and feel the utility of finding one perfectly suited to your needs. It's different. It may well be the future of commerce. If you decide to purchase an Android-powered tablet computer instead of an iPod or an iPad or a smart phone, Google's Android marketplace is another excellent way to experience the app world. Absorbing this now is crucial to preparing for later.

Peripherals

Peripherals are simply computer accoutrements, devices that add to the utility of a computer but are not necessary for its primary function – printers, cameras, microphones, scanners and game controllers. The volume and variety of options here is huge, and certainly, collect as many toys as you like. However, USB-powered mug-warming hotplates (yes, this is real) aside, there are a few key peripherals every professional of the digital age should have.

Webcam

Whether it's to video conference with colleagues halfway across the globe, record a talking head video entry for your blog or just keep in touch with friends and family using Skype, webcams are too useful and too cheap not to own. They come standard on most new laptops or as inexpensive add-ons for PCs that don't already have them built in. It's a must-have feature, so look for it when you are shopping for new hardware.

Microphone

Obviously, you'll want audio for your video. Almost any new webcam will include its own mic. Unfortunately, the audio quality on these is usually abysmal. This may suffice for a virtual catch-up with Aunt Suzie, but reflects poorly during webinar presentations with potential clients or when recording a podcast series to build your personal brand. Consider investing in an upgrade. Just bear in mind that audio devices uncannily reflect their price points; generally, you get what you pay for.

Wireless Router

Chances are, you already have a wireless Internet connection set up at home. The utility of having a personal WiFi connection for you and your family is undeniable and has become a pervasive aspect of digital life. Notoriously tricky to set up and laden with geek-speak jargon, WiFi connections are often neglected until they stop working, and they are rarely optimized for the best possible performance. Not only is this an unfortunate digital productivity suck, it may be a huge security threat. Truthfully, the majority of issues can be resolved with just three quick assessments.

1. First and foremost, is your wireless network secure? Have you added a password requirement for anyone who wants to log onto your wireless network? If not, your neighbors thank you for the free ride. Slightly less obvious: have you changed the default log-in information for administrator access to your router? If not, a tech-savvy person could do you *incredible* damage. To fix these problems, you'll need to log into the router itself. This can be accomplished by typing your router's IP address into the address bar of a web browser. If you don't know your router's IP address, you can find it by typing "ipconfig" in the Command prompt (in the Accessories folder) in Windows or "ifconfig" in the Terminal window (in the Utilities folder) in Mac OS. Your router's IP address is the number set displayed after the words "Default Gateway" (Windows) or "inet" (Mac). Enter this IP address into a web browser. This will direct you to the web interface for your router and ask for log-in information. Usually, leaving this blank allows you to continue; if not, search Google for your router's default log-in information. **This is the most common household security breach: Your router's default login information (username and password) can be found by doing a quick Google search!** Once logged in, ensure your wireless network requires a password to log in and change the router's default administrator log-in information to something else. Each brand of router works slightly differently on this, but should be intuitive enough. And if you get stuck, take heart: plenty of people have encountered the exact problem you have. Think digital! Google it or look for a video on YouTube.

DIGITAL DICTIONARY

IP address (Internet protocol address):

The numerical label assigned to all digital devices using the Internet. The most commonly used format is a set of four numbers separated by three periods (e.g., 192.168.1.1).

2. Now that your network is secure, is it optimized? There are a lot of settings, tweaks and hacks very geeky people will toy with to get the most juice out of their wireless network. I won't bore you with those. By far, the most important thing to check is which 802.11 protocol you are using. The 802.11 protocol is simply a set of standards that dictate how wireless communication is carried out. The possible protocols come in four flavors: 802.11a, 802.11b, 802.11g and 802.11n. When logged into your router, find the section containing wireless settings and look for an option for mode or protocol. The more simultaneous protocols used, the better, and generally, the higher the

letter, the better. This statement comes with two caveats. First, 802.11n was only released in 2009, and while it is *much* better than all the others, it may not work with all of your wireless-connected devices. Second, while 802.11b and 802.11g are more advanced protocols than 802.11a, they receive interference from other devices that operate on the same frequency, like microwaves, Bluetooth devices, cordless phones and two-way radios. Try testing different protocols, running an Internet connectivity speed test (www.speedtest.net/) to see which gets the best result.

3. Finally, does your network have enough coverage? Often, areas of the home physically distant or obstructed from the router receive weak or no wireless coverage. Arguably, the basement half-bath is the room that needs WiFi the most! This problem is solved with neat little devices called wireless repeaters. As the name suggests, they "repeat" your router's wireless signal, boosting the strength and range of your wireless network. This is a great, inexpensive and easy way to boost your wireless network and cover those pesky "dead" areas.

An important WiFi note: WiFi is not a substitute for a wired connection. When transferring big files (like movies) around your home network, even an 802.11n device wirelessly connected to an 802.11n router will be significantly slower than a wired connection. Keep that in mind when setting up your home office.

Scanner

For generations, we have suffered the grinding, constant frustration of desks covered in paper, envelopes stuffed with receipts and unusable, labyrinthine filing systems that snack on last year's tax returns. Why then do we still manage paperwork the same way our grandparents did? Opening the mail over the garbage, desperately saving the important bits while searching for pens, running out of stamps and losing the checkbook – we are stuck in a sorry mélange of pulp and paper cuts.

No more.

Scanners, those wonderful print-to-pixel machines, are the answer. Specifically, scanners that offer a combination of hardware and software that are "one-button" solutions. Many can scan both sides of a document and create an automatically named Adobe Acrobat (.PDF) file. These scanners feel magical. Using Optical Character Reading (OCR) software, all scanned text becomes searchable. Now, if you can't find something, simply type some keywords into your computer's search box, and in seconds every document that matches shows up. Need a utilities bill for proof of address at the DMV? Trying to remember the name of that great hotel you stayed at last year in London? Can't recall how much that furniture you donated to Salvation Army was credited for? All are now just a few keystrokes away. Digitize bank statements, paid bills, payment confirmations, RSVP requests, check stubs, stockholder reports and everything else you'd like to save, tuck the digital files away in hierarchal folders and toss the original. Of course, the whole world isn't paperless yet, and it's necessary to hold onto hard copies of a few things (tax documents, marriage certificates, etc.).

Now, multipage duplex scanners are not new. There are great units available from Fjitsu, HP, Xerox and Brother that come bundled with Adobe Acrobat at reasonable prices. Going paperless will dramatically increase the accuracy of your record keeping and save you so much time I know you'll never look back.

External Storage

Now that your house is in digital order, don't let it burn down. With the sum of your entire fiscal, legal and otherwise important transactions nestled lovingly on a hard drive, be aware of this one immutable digital fact: all drives fail. It might be in two days, two weeks or two years. It might be from age, defect or virus. But it will happen and it will probably happen at the most inconvenient time possible. It's heartbreaking enough to lose stored photos, music and videos, but losing critical paperwork is a full-on digital disaster. Spare yourself the pain. Invest in an external hard drive and perform regular backups of your system. External storage is dirt cheap, so there is no excuse on this one.

Photo Editing

A picture's ability to communicate is astounding. Photographs move humanity to action on the weightiest of global affairs – wars, elections, humanitarian crises – yet are also some of our most intimate, personal and prized possessions. Digital technology has so democratized this medium that dark rooms and negative film feel nearly as foreign as ink wells and quill pens. You *must* be fluent in this medium. Digital photography manipulation is too powerful, too simple and too inexpensive for you not to be. While artists and technical wizards can create aesthetics that most can never hope to contend with, every working professional should know how to execute four critical photographic techniques. Any photo editing software worth its salt will feature these core functions. It doesn't matter which software you use (suggestions: Photoshop, iPhoto, GIMP, Picasa); just understand why these concepts are important and how to execute them.

Crop

One of the most basic but endlessly useful manipulations, cropping a photo simply means cutting undesired portions out of an image. Trim images to focus on the subject, lose "undesirables" from the background, better fit within a blog post or match online specifications. Attention spans are limited on the web; don't waste an opportunity to connect with superfluous space in your images.

Border

Adding a border not only adds a level of polish to an image, but also serves a particularly useful purpose when it comes to email. Many different email interfaces will strip unnecessary data from messages to ease transfer and prevent malicious content from spreading. Unfortunately, this can wreak havoc on the display of a carefully formatted newsletter. Images that had been purposefully inlayed are now mashed right next to the text. Solve this issue by adding a border on the image itself. Simply create a 5-pixel-wide white border around the whole image, and voila: a fixed separation from any nearby text. It's probably a good idea to use this technique in blog posts as well. Sure, almost any blog software can add space between images and text that will display correctly on any web browser, but should the blog ever transfer to another platform or website, that formatting may be lost. Then you're presented with the fun choice of fixing each post individually – a massive, manual headache – or living with a blog archive full of ugly posts.

Exposure

One of the most common problems an amateur photographer runs into is exposure. An underexposed photo is too dark, while an overexposed photo appears washed out and too bright. While it's easier to deal with underexposure, photo editing software can digitally alter the exposure of a photograph, turning a nearly indecipherable image into a great candid. Alternatively, exposure can be toyed with to achieve all sorts of lurid aesthetics. Exposure is really easy to manipulate: simply move the slider in your editing software until the photo looks best to you.

DPI

DPI stands for dots per inch and refers to the measurement of printing dot density placed along a one-inch-long line. In simpler terms, think of it as a measure of image quality: more dots mean better-looking images. This should not be confused with an image's resolution, which is often expressed as a measurement of pixels in height and width, and can (imperfectly) be thought of as an image's native size. In practice, all you need to remember is that photo editing software can export an image at various DPI, and depending on where the image will be, certain DPI are best. Thankfully, this basically comes down to three numbers to remember. Images should be exported at specific levels for specific mediums:

- Images for display on the web should be exported at 72 DPI.
- Images for display over fax should be exported at 144 DPI.
- Images for display in printed material should be exported at 300 DPI.

These are the upper limit of what each medium can actually display and what the human eye can actually perceive. Anything more is wasted data; anything less is suboptimal. Just remember: once an image is created at a lower DPI, it can't then be re-exported at a higher DPI; that information was lost. This is why it's important to keep the raw file of any image you may want to use for multiple purposes.

Video Editing

People shoot and upload a lot of video, and they're doing it more and more every day.

Digital video is the future. The broadcasting and cable industry knows this. Hollywood knows this. You need to know this. And not in the "I know that dinosaurs existed in the Mesozoic Era" kind of way. Know this like you know the old baseball injury in your right knee hurts when it rains.

The power and reach of online video are unassailable. The moving image has been the palette and platform of choice for the storytelling maestros of the past few decades, but digital technology has democratized the process, offering everyone the spotlight long reserved for the well-connected, well-financed and well-trained.

In short, the ball is in your court. Certainly, the average Joe doesn't need the skill of a postproduction professional, but whether it's to trim the fat from a personal branding webcast, add text to the video tour of a new franchise location or just sweeten those home movies with some special effects, everyone should possess basic video editing skills. The basic application of the techniques listed below can be achieved with simple, free programs like Apple's iMovie and Windows Movie Maker – both bundled with their respective OS – or third-party software such as Premiere Express and JayCut. Overachievers may want to try to tackle full-featured premium programs like Final Cut Pro, Avid or Premiere, but beware: for those unfamiliar with video editing, these programs can be overwhelming; expect a steep learning curve. Regardless of your software choice, you need to be comfortable executing the following techniques.

Video Editorial Strategy

The technical side of video production has three parts:

1. **Acquisition** (shooting or obtaining video source material)
2. **Editorial** (getting the video into your computer, editing it together and outputting it to a master file)
3. **Distribution** (uploading the file to a distribution system [like YouTube] or making DVDs or other distributable media)

But before you start ingesting video and cutting together segments, it is a good idea to think about what you're trying to do. Professionals call it "production concept." It can be anything, for example, "We're going to make a sales film" or "I want to make a photo montage for my brother's wedding anniversary party." Or even "Let's make an instructional video." It doesn't matter what your production concept is. What matters is that you understand what you are trying to create and stick to the concept.

The language of video is very similar to spoken language, and video stories are built very much in the same way as spoken or written stories. Videos have beginnings, middles and endings. They have rising action, a climax and falling action. There should be a story arch that you can outline on paper.

You don't have to be a professional screen writer, and you don't need to know any special jargon. Write down what you want to accomplish in the form of a script or shot sheet. It can be as simple as:

1. Take an opening shot of the outside of your building.
2. Take lots of extra shots (called B-Roll) of the door and walkway and do a few quick pans to use as transition shots.

DIGITAL DICTIONARY

B-Roll:

In the early days of filmmaking, the A-Roll was the roll of film with the primary action on it. The B-Roll was the roll of film with the insert shots and reaction shots on it, for example, interviewer head nods or product shots. Sometimes both A- Roll and B-Roll are shot with two different cameras (A & B), and other times all the shots are done with one camera and in no particular sequence. Today, B-Roll is slang for any shots you can use to move your story along or cover your mistakes. In practice, you can never shoot too much B-Roll.

3. Shoot the narrator reading the opening monologue.

4. Et cetera.

Write something simple, treat each shot as a task and cross it off your list after it is shot. Stick to your production concept, stick to your script and make sure you've told your story. Here are a few techniques that will help you.

Acquisition

Shooting video is an art. But there are some simple rules you can keep in mind that will help you tell better stories.

1)   Be aware of your light source. Can you see the action you are covering clearly? If it's a sunny day, are the faces in shadows? Being aware of the clarity of your main subjects will always yield better results.

2)   Start your shot early and leave it late. Professionals call this head trim and tail trim. It is the number of seconds of video before and after the main action of your scene. The longer it is, the happier you will be. Especially if you need to dissolve into the scene from another one. A good rule of thumb is start shooting three to four seconds before you call action and hold the end of every shot for at least the count of three.

3)   Take your time with every shot. Resist the temptation to move from subject to subject as if you were looking around the room. Hold every shot for enough time. Sometimes you should describe the scene to yourself as you shoot and not move the camera until you have finished. If you have a script and will describe the scene with a voiceover for the final production, make sure you have timed the read or read it to yourself while you are shooting. Overshoot! You can never shoot enough video for a project.

4)   Don't be afraid to move. Taking time with a shot does not mean making it static. If your subject is moving, move with it. Follow the action. It will make your video feel more contemporary. That said, if you are shooting talking heads in chairs or at desks, use a tripod to steady the camera. There is nothing more disconcerting or annoying than gratuitous or extraneous camera movements.

Ingesting Video

After you shoot your video, you are going to need to ingest it into a video editing system. This is sometimes called uploading, encoding or transcoding. They are the wrong words for the action, but they are commonly used to describe the process. Your video editing software will have a specific method that is best for taking video from your camera and putting it on your hard drive so it can be edited. This seemingly simple process is the subject of hundreds of books, thousands of websites and millions of blog posts. I won't try to cover it here. If you are new to video production, just follow the directions included with your editing software.

Cuts

The simplest editing action is cutting from scene to scene. This is sometimes called a butt-splice or a hard cut. Cuts are used more than any other type of video transition. There is a reason: if they are done correctly, people don't notice them.

In ancient times (20 years ago), editors had to physically cut the film and manually remove undesired frames and then splice the strip back together using Rube Goldberg contraptions that looked like a cross between film projectors and pinball machines. This process is now accomplished with a few mouse clicks and keystrokes.

Of course, the technical aspect of cutting is the easy part. The artistry of it is where the real action is. Just like painting, singing and dancing, video editing is an art. It's difficult to teach or describe, and at a certain point, either you have a knack for it or you don't. It's about making smart selections from the raw footage, laying clips together at a gratifying pace, placing shots and scenes next to each other in clever, unexpected ways and ensuring the entire piece flows together, forming a cohesive narrative the audience can understand. If this sounds like a lot to take in (and it is), start by learning a fun new term to drop at cocktail parties: beats. The jargon of storytellers, a beat is a unit of narrative that advances the story and shapes the turning of a scene. Beats are the countless little dominoes that fall through every movie, television show, paperback fiction and play ever created.

The dog sees a balloon (beat). The dog pounces on the balloon (beat). The balloon explodes (beat). The dog runs away whimpering, tail between its knees (beat).

Simple as that example may be, the beats within it represent the structural core of every story ever told. Lifetimes are spent pursuing the mastery of beats, and video editing relies on their manipulation. As a beginner, focus on ensuring every cut contains a beat that pushes your story forward. Don't keep uneventful shots in the video. Don't repeat or linger on a beat already made. Always progress; always present new information. That is the most basic maxim of cutting video.

Much, much more can be said on this topic, but unless you're aiming for a career in Hollywood, this is enough. In fact, whether you're cutting together a short version of a live webinar, creating a simple product demonstration or just trying to add a little polish to that home movie before it goes up on YouTube, a "good enough" edit is probably a dramatic improvement over the raw footage. Ninety percent of the time, this is a perfectly acceptable solution and one you can achieve on your own. For the other 10% – those high-profile or ROI-dependent projects – hiring a professional is probably the best way to go.

Dissolves

Most of the time, you will cut between scenes, especially when the action takes place simultaneously or sequentially. If you want to show the passage of time, however, a dissolve or cross-fade is the transition of choice. Dissolves can be done in almost any length from super short to several seconds. Don't overuse dissolves; people quickly tire of them.

Soft Cuts

One favorite trick of professional editors is the soft cut. It is a very fast dissolve (under four video frames). You often see soft cuts used to smooth out a transition between two almost identical shots (like a talking head) when you don't have B-Roll to cover the video you are editing out.

Additional Transitions

Although dissolves, cuts and soft cuts are transitions, there are many others. In fact, there are literally thousands of special effects transitions that you can apply when moving from shot to shot. Abbreviations vary. Some people call them SFX (special effects); others call them EFX (effects). No matter what you call them, when one shot ends and another shot begins, it is possible to use a transition.

The *vast* majority of your transitions should be cuts. Inexperienced editors often overuse special effects transitions, making their video look silly and amateurish. However, a well-placed transition can really help cover up problem cuts that don't mix well together, better pace disparate scenes or add an artistic touch to your video.

There are hundreds of possible transitions: flashes, freezes, slides and all sorts of special effects. Just use them sparingly. The more transitions used and the more jarring they are, the more likely a video is to come off as cheesy. One rule to live by: less is more.

Text

Adding text to video often conveys information that would be difficult to express in any other way. Titles and credits are the classic and ubiquitous example, but there are lots of other creative, useful ways to use text in video. Lower-thirds, or text superimposed on the lower third of the screen, are a great way to state the name and title of an interviewee currently on the screen. Sometimes, it makes sense to display nothing but text between video shots in order to contextualize or offer exposition on a scene. This is called using a title card, art card or text slate. It might be important to scroll a special warning or notice ("Do Not Try This at Home!") along the bottom of a scene. Just keep in mind that this is a video, not an article. Never tell the audience something you could show them instead. Always use economy of language, expressing yourself in as few words as possible. One quick trick: don't just cut to text; fade your text in and out. It's easy to do, and it will make your video productions look much more professionally produced.

Export

So, after hours of careful crafting, your video is ready to be seen by the world. The process of preparing a digital video for distribution is called exporting. There is a very good chance that you can just find the word "export" on the File menu and choose something simple, such as iPhone or web video. Video file exporting is getting simpler by the day.

The most critical decision made during the exporting process is which file format to export to. While there are lots of options, Quicktime (.MOV) using the H.264 CODEC is the best bet for most people in most situations. Quicktime files are the most widely viewable on the most platforms (notably, the iPhone and iPad) and can be uploaded to iTunes and YouTube, making them easily embeddable in blog posts and websites. There are good reasons to use other formats (namely,

DIGITAL DICTIONARY

CODEC:

A portmanteau (a blending of two or more words) of "compressor-decompressor" or, more commonly, "coder-decoder." In practice, a CODEC allows your computer to record or play back audio, video or still computer files. Popular CODECS include H.264, AAC and MPEG.

Flash), but unless you want to get heavy duty into online video distribution, Quicktime should serve you well enough. Regardless, *always* save a backup of the video project file and export an uncompressed version (called a master) of the video in case you need to re-export later.

HTML

HTML is the computer programming language of the World Wide Web. It stands for hyper-text markup language, and knowing just that puts you ahead of 90% of the population. But other than scoring extra points on trivia night, that won't get you very far. To truly thrive in the digital age, you'll need a more concrete, working knowledge of HTML.

There are several good reasons to master some HTML basics. First and foremost is to be able to look at a webpage and understand what it is, who wrote it, what metadata are being used, what keywords, and so on. This is hugely helpful (and a free tool) for executives who are trying to evaluate a competitor's website or gain some insights into what kind of SEO and SEM a given website is using.

Right now, go to any web browser and browse to any website you like – your site, a competitor's – it doesn't matter for this example. Click on the View menu (it doesn't matter what browser you are using; this is a universal feature of all browsers on all computers that can surf the web). Now click View Source or Page Source. Can you read what you see? What you are looking at is the actual web page written in HTML, the language of the World Wide Web. With very little knowledge and a small amount of practice, you will be able to read the important parts of a source page and use them to your advantage. Think it's too tough or too technical? Your competitors don't. You should be able to view the source of any webpage and speak intelligently about what you see there.

Of course, there is another good reason to learn a little HTML. It will make you a better and more efficient executive. You don't need to be fluent in HTML; there are a lot of professionals for hire better suited for that task. But you should be able to make small changes to your site without paying for them or asking for help. Crafting blog comments, emails and blog posts that let you stand out and be remembered is pretty simple. It's important to have a cursory understanding of a place you more than likely spend several hours at each day.

At its most basic, HTML works by instructing a web browser to manipulate text and images with the less than (<) and greater than (>) signs. The code within those signs is called a tag, and it performs a variety of functions. Many "wrap" around text and indicate a manipulation to that text, like this:

<p>This is just plain text</p>

In the above example, the <p> and </p> tags are telling the web browser to make the text within its own separate paragraph. Notice how the tag has an opening (<p>) and a closing (</p>). All closing tags are the same as the opening tag, with the forward slash character (/) at the start. Some tags stand alone and do not directly affect text, and as such do not require a closing tag, like this:

This is called a break tag, and it instructs the web browser to add a line break at that point in the text, much like the return key on a word processor. Once you grasp this fundamental principle, learning much of the rest of HTML is just learning different tags and how to use them.

This section is not intended to teach you how to code in HTML; there are many, many fantastic online reference guides available for that. In fact, Googling "HTML code" plus any common formatting action will return multiple results that demonstrate exactly how to code that particular task. Alternatively, www.quackit. com/html/codes is a great jumping-off point for most basic HTML functions.

In this way, just about anybody can code in HTML without really "knowing" HTML. For our purposes, I'd like to highlight a few key techniques and concepts every professional should have in a digital toolkit.

Formatting

Everyone should be able to code basic text formatting tasks in HTML. Sure, any blog or email client worth its salt has the ability to write in WYSIWYG (What You See Is What You Get) style, with a familiar word processor–style formatting bar on top. But what happens if you want to make a quick change to that blog post from your smartphone, which won't display the formatting bar? Or what if you want to turn that blog post into a static web page? What if you want to add clarity to a message board post or blog comment that doesn't have a formatting bar? What if your newsletter formatting breaks and you can't fix it without looking at the raw HTML?

It's just too easy and too useful not to know how to manage the basics; be able to **bold** (<b>), *italicize* (<i>), center-align text (<P align=center>), left-align text (<P align=left>) and right-align text (<P align=right>) in HTML. For bonus points, you may want to familiarize yourself with other common HTML formatting tags, like bigger font (<big>), smaller font (<small>), ~~strikethrough~~ (<s>), <u>underline</u> (<u>), block quotes (<blockquote>), bulleted lists (<ul> and <li>), numbered lists (<ol> and <li>) and more structural code like <head>, <h1> and <div>.

Linking

The web without links is no web at all. The HTML code for linking is quite simple: <a href="http://www.samplelink.com/">Link Text</a>. A lot of blog software will create HTML links just like this. When a reader clicks on such a link, the page currently being viewed (your blog post) goes away, and the page that the clicked link directed the reader to takes its place.

Wouldn't it be better if the link opened up another tab or window in your browser, as opposed to taking your audience to someone else's website? Of course it would. And now that you are learning the basics of HTML, you can fix this.

Just add a "_blank" to the link, like this:

<a href="http://www.samplelink.com/" target="_blank">Link Text</a>

That extra bit (target= "_blank") in the middle causes a clicked link to open in a new window or tab, a much better experience for your reader and for you.

There's other important stuff you can do with linking, or "hyperlinks," as they were known in the old days. Try making an HTML link in a blog post that automatically opens up the user's email software and automatically addresses an email to you. You already know the format:

<a href="mailto:address@gmail.com">Email Me</a>.

Images

I've stressed the importance of visual communication: people like pictures. You get it. Consequently, using HTML to display images is important. The code itself is fairly simple: <img src="image.gif" />

You are going to use this little piece of code almost every day. Whether it's to learn where an image is stored or to place an image on a site or a blogpost, do yourself a favor and learn how to use the <img src> tag.

Image Selection

Now, before moving on, we should spend a few words on image selection. I'm not referring to which image is used; that's subjective and a matter of situational taste. I'm talking about *where* an image comes from. Photographers, illustrators and artists work very hard to create a stunning array of visual content. Many of them generously upload their work to the web for everyone to admire. It is incredibly easy to right click on these images, save them to a hard drive and use them for your own purposes. This is called copyright infringement, or simply *stealing*. Don't do it.

Many of these image makers would happily grant you permission to use their work in exchange for proper accreditation. Just ask first. Barring that, there are huge pools of free visual content online. Many of the images on Flickr are managed under Creative Commons licenses, making them free to use, modify and share (within reason). Visit http://www.flickr.com/creativecommons to find out more about Creative Commons licenses and how to discover images managed under them on Flickr.

Beyond Flickr, many media and business entities release EPKs (electronic press kits) that contain copyright-free images and videos. Stock image houses offer royalty-free images for very modest prices, and a few, like FreeDigitalPhotos. net, offer some photos for free in exchange for accreditation. And don't forget: the advanced search function on Google Image search (http://www.google.com/imghp) lets you search web images, filtered by usage rights.

Cheat

OK, it's time we let you in on the secret. Almost nobody actually hand-codes full websites in HTML anymore. That stuff is complicated! Rather, a series of tools exist to ease the creation of HTML through WYSIWYG and other, more straightforward methods. Dreamweaver, part of Adobe's Creative Suite of software, is a market-leading option. Certainly, to tackle any serious

DIGITAL DICTIONARY

Creative Commons (CC):

A nonprofit organization that manages various copyright licenses that communicate the rights a content creator wishes to reserve, waive or alter.

website creation, you'll need a tool like Dreamweaver, Microsoft Expression Web or their equivalent.   But even for dabblers, using Dreamweaver and Expression to get actual HTML from WYSIWYG creations is an excellent way to learn, tweak and tinker.

Microsoft Office

Intimate to cubicle dwellers the world over, Microsoft Office (MS Office) is in the business of business. Its ubiquity is undeniable, and for good reason: they truly make the best-of-breed software for office work. It's rare that I'm not a champion of open source or online software solutions, but there really aren't competitive options for heavy-duty document writing, spreadsheet creation and (to an extent) presentation making. I *love* Google Documents (web-based office software) for a variety of reasons, but if you're trying to write a novel or compile a yearly sales report, it's just not the same as Microsoft Word. More importantly, a large percentage of the offices in the world use MS Office. Developing "mad Office skills" will not only make you more efficient, it will make you more marketable. At the very least, all working professionals should have a few Office tricks up their sleeve.

Word

Chances are, you're pretty comfortable with Word already, formatting text, changing fonts, bulleting lists and the like. This is a good baseline, but more advanced functions can help in a variety of situations. I won't get into the specifics of how to achieve these tasks – they're a bit different in each version of the software. Simply use the Help function in the program for step-by-step instructions on how to accomplish these tasks in your version of Word.

To begin, any time you're collaborating with other people on a document, use Word's Track Changes function. When Track Changes mode is on, any edits made to a document don't permanently alter the text, but rather make redline editor's marks on the suggested change. Your colleague can then accept or reject those changes one by one, making the process a truer collaboration, rather than just a version passing exercise in "my turn." In this review mode, it's also possible to make sidelined comments on specifically marked sections of the document, allowing specific discussion, rather than general notes.

When tackling especially lengthy works, using the Document Map function is awesome. The Document Map displays an outline structural view of the document in a left-hand sidebar next to the document itself. By using hierarchical outline tags (special fonts) for key chapters, headings and subheadings, even extremely large documents, like yearly reports and novels, can be easily navigated and digested by multiple parties.

When it comes to the bowels of the writing itself, go beyond simple text-formatting functions and ensure you can manipulate page layout functions. Specifically, be able to modify the page margins, page orientation (vertical portrait vs. horizontal landscape) and line spacing; add a page break (very useful for multipage documents that need clear section separation) or separate the text into any number of columns for newspaper- and newsletter-style layouts. Also, make sure you can insert images, tables and graphs into your document while maintaining this kind of page formatting.

Of course, never reinvent the wheel if you don't have to! It's shocking how many people forget or ignore the prebuilt templates in Word. Every time you create a new document in Word, you're prompted to create either a blank document or one from a template. There are literally hundreds of preinstalled and downloadable templates created by function-minded designers. Using Word templates, you can create cover letters, contracts, purchase orders, résumés, postcards, fax sheets, memos, agendas, calendars and other everyday documents in minutes.

Finally, use keyboard shortcuts for everything. If it's something you do with only relative frequency, it has a shortcut, and the time it saves will far outweigh the modest homework it takes to learn and use it. Just about everybody can benefit from shortcutting with the following Windows shortcuts (Mac users substitute the Command key for the Ctrl key):

- Undo: Ctrl-Z
- Redo: Ctrl-Y
- Copy: Ctrl-C
- Paste: Ctrl-V
- Bold: Ctrl-B
- Italicize: Ctrl-I
- Underline: Ctrl-U
- Jump cursor by word: Ctrl-Left or Right Arrow
- Select with cursor: Shift-Left or Right Arrow

- Select word with cursor: Ctrl-Shift-Left or Right Arrow
- Delete word preceding cursor: Ctrl-Delete
- Left adjust: Ctrl-L
- Right adjust: Ctrl-R
- Center adjust: Ctrl-E
- Find: Ctrl-F
- Check spelling and grammar: F7
- Thesaurus: Shift-F7
- Save: Ctrl-S
- Open: Ctrl-O
- Print: Ctrl-P

Learn them, use them and love them. You'll like how much time you save, and you'll love how much better your wrist feels.

Excel

Excel is too often viewed as the domain of bean counters and data dorks. Useful as a workaday number cruncher and designer-on-demand for the visual display of quantitative information, Excel should really be something you are comfortable using. Hopefully you've at least opened the program before, entered a few numbers and maybe even cleaned up the spreadsheet with a little formatting. It's time, then, to step up, skill up and head down the power use path. Again, each yearly version of Excel modifies how to go about each of these activities, but any version's Help function along with some Google work will facilitate your ability to execute them.

Excel, like all spreadsheet programs, was originally designed to replace a paper spreadsheet that was commonly used by accountants and scientists to foot and cross-foot rows and columns of numbers. This is a quaint metaphor maybe for what the original program was designed to do, but a current version of Excel is a powerful computational tool with extraordinary databasing and formatting capabilities.

Formulas

Formulas are the core function of Excel, enabling spreadsheets to automatically process complex modifications of data. Instructions on how to create formulas are widely available in the Help section of the software and on the web, but each formula begins in the same way, with an equal sign (=). The magic of Excel is the reference cell. This simply means that you use a reference cell name, such as "A3," instead of a static number. This allows the spreadsheet to become a dynamic document, modifying a complex string of variables by changing just one input.

The most common type of formula is computational: sum, subtract, multiply, divide or find the mean, median and mode from a set of data. Beyond this simple arithmetic, Excel can compute far more advanced mathematical concepts such as trigonometry, statistics, financial modeling and engineering functions. In support of this computation, Excel can also handle logical and conditional execution, such as returning one set of data over another given Boolean conditions. It can even search data sets and return specific figures based on a variety of requests, for example, return the highest or lowest number, count the blank cells or count the numbers greater or less than a set number. It can convert feet to meters, Celsius to Fahrenheit and everything in between. It can manipulate text inputs in all manner of ways, add the date and time to an input or serve you breakfast (not really).

In short, Excel can do a lot. Probably a lot more than you think it can. Google a "list of Excel formulas" to explore the extent.

Macros

Separate from a formula is a macro. An Excel macro is simply a set of commands and functions that can be stored and set up for one-click automation. Do you find yourself continually performing a common set of tasks in Excel? Maybe it's a series of visual formats frequently applied or regular data sets that are always organized and analyzed in the same way. Macros are a great way to store these common tasks for easy repetition later. On the higher end, macros can become quite complex, but simple macros can be created through a process in which Excel records all the keystrokes and actions you perform and compiles them into a single action which can be repeated later.

Formatting

Of course, the mountain of raw data that macros and formulas create isn't very useful unless it is presented clearly and cleanly. Familiar manipulations such as bolding and text alignment are available in Excel and dramatically increase the readability of a spreadsheet, but certain Excel-specific design functions matter even more. Be sure you understand how to merge cells so that conjoining cells become one large cell, a useful way to clarify column and table headings. Be conscious of the choice to show gridlines or not; some areas of the spreadsheet are far more readable with visible gridlines; some are less so. Use cell shading (changing the background color of a cell) liberally to contrast dense data sets or highlight various sections of the spreadsheet.

Sorting

Excel's sort function is incredibly useful. It's an action that ranks data in ascending or descending order either numerically or alphabetically. Finally, just like Word, Excel comes packaged with a huge variety of designed templates – everything from invoices and agendas to fax cover sheets and stationery. Don't do work you don't have to.

Security

With these basic skills, you can easily create beautiful, practical, convenient spreadsheets full of wildly sensitive, confidential information. Maybe it's full of sales data, salary information and proprietary algorithms. Or maybe you just don't want people futzing around with your painstakingly constructed spreadsheet. Mercifully, Excel has a number of different ways to protect and otherwise conceal data. First, you must protect a spreadsheet in the Tools menu, optionally requiring a password to open the workbook. A protected spreadsheet can lock down specific cells so they are unalterable – a useful technique for guarding formulas from modification. You can also hide specific cells so the data remain but are not viewable or printable. Just bear in mind that this is not CIA-level security. The encryption code used to protect an Excel document is fairly rudimentary, and passwords are breakable. Determined espionage will not be stopped. If the data within a document are of paramount secrecy, don't rely on Excel protection to keep them safe. Use Excel's protection functions more as a safeguard against accidental vandalism and as basic security due diligence.

Finally, many of the data generated in an Excel document are difficult to digest in raw form. Besides, everyone loves a good pie graph. Use the automatic chart generator to create charts and graphs of all kinds: line, bar, area, bubble and, yes, pie. Many of these graphs can be three-dimensionally rendered to put that final bit of polish on a report headed upstairs. Just don't forget to add contextualizing information such as graph titles, x/y axis labels and a legend.

PowerPoint

It is my belief that people who use PowerPoint should be trained, tested and federally licensed! We have all suffered the quiet, intolerable despair of a terrible PowerPoint presentation. Some are the stuff of legends, stories of horror recounted at trade conventions and five-o-clock meetings everywhere. Don't become the subject of one of these cautionary tales. With only a little effort and foresight, any presentation can be a lively, engaging exercise in communication.

Truthfully, there are two types of PowerPoint decks: a printed leave-behind and the proper presentation. The leave-behind can contain a lot more detail and text and should be offered *after* you give a presentation to your audience. Your proper presentation deck should be minimal in detail and visually dynamic – pictures are far better than text. If you need more than a few bullet points or images to help keep your thoughts organized and your presentation moving, find time to better memorize it. Under no circumstances should you be reading from a PowerPoint presentation being delivered live. This is a public speaking exercise, not a public reading one.

Use PowerPoint for public speaking, not public reading!

To begin, we'll depart slightly from our premise that Microsoft makes the best office software. While PowerPoint is an industry standard and has evolved into a more capable program in recent years, it pales in comparison to Apple's presentation software, Keynote. Apple just does media content creation better across the board, presentations included. Keynote is not only more intuitive to use, it creates a slicker, more aesthetically pleasing set of slides. As an added bonus, an application in the app store called Keynote Remote allows the control of Keynote slides on your computer with an iPhone or iPod Touch. Of course, if you want to download the Apple Wireless mouse app and use your iPhone or iPod Touch as a wireless mouse to control your Mac, 10,000 style points for you.

As much as I love Keynote, I have to admit that in this one, small instance, Macs and PCs are not fully compatible. While it is true that you can output a Keynote file in PowerPoint format, some of the more advanced features of Keynote do not translate to PowerPoint, and this can cause some serious issues when you are presenting on someone else's computer. That said, when you are going to use your own Mac to present, go ahead and use Keynote – it's a better program.

Templates

In just about every case, starting with a presentation template makes sense. The included templates or third-party templates created by professional designers pay special attention to consistency of backgrounds, fonts, styles and color schemes. I like more minimalist designs, but choose whatever suits your style. Tweak individual elements as you see fit, but using a template as a starting point is almost always faster than conjuring up a presentation from scratch. That said, if you do have the skills to create your own template or even just a customized master slide, it will really add polish to your presentation.

Presentation Strategy

There are two main types of presentation decks: (1) speaker support and (2) leave-behind. Do everyone on earth a favor and know which kind of deck you are creating.

Speaker Support

To create a deck to support your presentation, consider not doing a deck at all. You know your business, you know your topic – do you really need the audience looking at something while you are trying to communicate with them? If the answer is yes, consider what type of visuals makes sense. A picture is worth a thousand words. Use as many of them as possible. A big image that is related to the point you are trying to cover is preferable to a page full of 12-point type that no one in the audience can read. Try adding a caption or a text cloud for fun. If you need to do straight text, here is my ironclad rule: Maximum of four bullets per page (three is preferable), minimum font size 36 points (40 is preferable). You will immediately notice that this rule leaves you almost no room on the page. Yep! Deal with it. You will have short bullet points that you *will not read!* You will talk about the bullet points, but you will never, ever read them from the stage.

Notes

If not having all the relevant talking points at hand makes you nervous, use the software's presenter notes feature to display information on the presentation computer but not on the display monitor. Again, it really can't be stressed enough how superior visuals are for expressing information in a presentation. Be sure you can add visual elements to a presentation with flare: insert pictures with various layouts and effects, use the "build" technique to create the appearance of movement on your graphs and add audio/visual elements to break up the flow and give your voice a rest. Finally, use slide transitions for a little pizzazz or to punctuate key slides. Similar to video transitions, a little goes a long way here. Don't overdo it, or your presentation will quickly degrade into a laughable, tacky mess.

The Leave-Behind Deck

Truthfully, the trick to a good presentation isn't in the software; it's in you. If you're creating a PowerPoint or Keynote document as a piece of collateral to be sent out rather than physically presented, you're using the wrong software. Make a PDF or get a designer to mock up something in Adobe InDesign instead. At its best, presentation software is used to make presentations (duh), and the most important piece of that equation is the presenter – you.

Be a Pro!

Always arrive at least 15–30 minutes ahead of time to arrange the room, set up the projector/display monitor and troubleshoot any technical issues (there's always one), leaving you cool and collected come show time. If you are using a laptop, bring an AC cord, as battery power has a nasty way of running out mid-presentation.

The World Is Your Stage

One-to-many communication is an art form. Are you speaking to two people huddled around your laptop, a small group in a conference room, 20 people in a big conference room, 500 people in an auditorium? You will use a different tone of voice and different presentation skills in each situation. You already know how to talk to small groups; you've been doing it all of your life. But a presentation is not the same as telling your family about your recent vacation – oh, wait, yes it is! The keys to great public speaking are honesty, integrity, belief in yourself, belief in your topic and absolute knowledge of your subject matter. When you know your work, it's easy to make eye contact and speak in an authoritative but relaxed voice. Remember, passion for your topic is infectious. People love to listen to people who are passionate when they speak. Is it hard to speak passionately about the adjusted case volume of widgets in Q1 year over year? No. Not to people who care about that subject. Trust me: when you speak about widget sales to the sales manager whose bonus is directly tied to the numbers you're presenting, you will command attention.

Of course, modify what you have to say to fit the room. And if you have a handout (a separately created leave-behind deck), save it until the presentation is over. With something in their hands, your audience will be focused on it and not on you.

Practice Does Not Make Perfect – Perfect Practice Makes Perfect!

Above all, practice the presentation ahead of time so you convey your points confidently and comfortably. If the thought of public speaking sends incorporeal spiders crawling up your spine, join a club that offers a low-stakes opportunity to get comfortable with the idea, like Toastmasters or an improv comedy workshop. Some of the best presentations in the world are made at the annual TED (Technology, Entertainment, Design) Conference through the now-famous forum, TED Talks (www.ted.com/talks). Watch and learn from these masters. You might even try searching YouTube for presentations on topics that interest you. You'll watch some that go over quite well; mimic them. You'll watch some that don't; learn from their mistakes.

With just a bit of practice and planning, you'll find presentations an enlivening, not excruciating, experience for all involved.

Chapter 9:
Small Office / Home Office

Those who have embraced the entrepreneurial spirit know all too well the challenges of making a go of business sans the trappings of dedicated brick and mortar, but even those mired in the corporate world often find themselves in need of a small office / home office (SoHo). Whether it's the start of your own LLC, living quarters for a side project or simply dedicated space adapted for personal business, a SoHo is more than a luxury in the digital age. These enclaves of personal productivity are an absolute necessity for any serious undertaking and a serious boon for any working professional. Certainly, tailor your SoHo to suit your unique personal needs, add organically as those needs grow, and don't overdo. As with most advice in this book, creating your own SoHo is an opportunity to self-invest and pull away from the professional pack.

Connect

Without the web, the modern workplace nearly grinds to a halt. Before getting into specifics on how to best get a SoHo online, it might help to have some basic definitions and a working understanding of how we actually connect to the wonder that is the Internet. Let's review some technobabble.

Broadband

To start, what exactly is broadband? The technical definition is "responding to or operating at a wide band of frequencies." This is a bit cryptic. In practice, people use the term to describe a robust Internet connection, a fast wireless connection or any connection to the Internet that's faster than an old-fashioned dial-up. You may simply think of it as a very fast, high-capacity way to access the web. How fast is fast enough? No matter how fast your connection is, you are always going to need a faster one. Purchase the highest-speed Internet connectivity you can reasonably afford. It will make everything about your digital life better.

Contention

Now, how fast is fast? Broadband speed is measured in megabits per second, and offered connection speeds vary wildly. Those connections' quoted specifications also vary widely, based on another important, new vocabulary word: contention. Your ISP (Internet Service Provider) may sell you a six-megabit-per-second connection, but if you try to browse the Internet at 9 PM, you might find your actual speeds are far slower. That's due to contention: how many people are contending for the same bandwidth? Finally, know that most connections are not symmetrical. It is very rare for ISPs to offer a consumer connection where the download speed and the upload speed are the same. Symmetrical connections are available, but they are usually business products. At home, you are likely to be offered an asymmetrical service such as six megabits per second down and one megabit per second up. Why do you care about upload capacity? Well, do you want to transfer videos, documents and other files to other computers or a cloud server? Do you want to use one of the popular cloud-based backup systems? The slower your upload connection, the more time it will take.

Bits and Bytes

So, what's the difference between a megabit and a megabyte? A bit is the smallest unit of information that can be stored or manipulated on a computer; it consists of either a one or a zero. A bit is not just the smallest unit of information a computer can handle; it's also the largest. So, to make their lives easier, programmers commonly bunch bits into eight-bit bytes. The math is very simple: 1 byte equals 8 bits. Now, when you want to describe a million of something, you add the prefix "mega" to it. So a million bits is a megabit. Megabits are abbreviated Mbps (notice the small "b"); megabytes are abbreviated MBps or simply MB (notice the big "B"); therefore: 1 MBps (megabyte) = 8 Mbps (megabits). Of course, nothing in the computer business is ever that simple. Networking hardware (network cards and routers) is typically rated in Mbps (megabits). Confusingly, most computer peripherals (hard disks and memory) are rated in MBps (megabytes).

Bits and Bytes
1 byte = 8 bits
1 megabit (abbrev. Mbps) = 1,000,000 bits
1 megabyte (abbrev. MBps or MB) = 1,000,000 bytes

No problem; now you know how to do the math. To upload a 100 MB file from your computer to a remote hard disk, your network connection would need to process 800 Mbps of data. So, in a perfect world with no contention, a 3-megabit-up connection would take just over 266 seconds (800 Mbps / 3 Mbps per second) to upload. Since we don't even *rate* storage devices in megabytes anymore but in gigabytes (GB), and 1 GB equals 1,000 MB, you can see how much time a speedy broadband connection saves when transferring files of size with any frequency.

Getting Connected

So, with a few ten-dollar tech words in your pocket and the math to back them up, you're likely asking the real question: what kind of connection should I get? It goes without saying, the faster the better, but since prices scale with speed, consider your actual needs. If you have just one or two people working out of the space without a terribly intense need to transfer large files online, a typical healthy residential connection of 3-25 Mbps down and 1-5 Mbps up will likely suffice. If there are several people working simultaneously, if you plan to host your own content on an in-house server or if you will be transferring a lot of data across the web, consider investing in a heftier, potentially symmetrical connection of 45 Mbps such as a T-3. Your ISP can assist you with information on your current connection and the pricing of upgrades. Or, alternatively, you may be able to obtain a high-speed consumer service from your cable company over a DOCSIS 3 cable modem or via fiber optic cables from your phone company.

Regardless, as with all things digital, this space is growing constantly. Occasionally, take stock of your connection versus the new "normal" sold by your ISP. If warranted – that is, if you find yourself frustrated by how slow websites load, how long emails take to download, or how long your online backup is taking – invest in an upgrade.

Wired vs. Wireless

Don't sabotage your broadband connection by falling prey to a common error – going 100% wireless. I love WiFi. I hope you do too. I really hope you followed my advice from the last chapter to secure, optimize and fully cover your own home WiFi network. Just don't become fully dependent on it. Make sure every working person in your SoHo has access to an Ethernet cord (using Cat 5e cable or better). While WiFi is incredibly convenient, it's not nearly as effective as a traditional online link; a wired connection can be up to ten times faster than a wireless one. You will really notice this when transferring files around the office. Don't outpace everyone else with a high-speed connection only to cut yourself off at the knees.

As a final word on connectivity, let's talk about connecting remotely. Even the most reclusive SoHo dweller must emerge occasionally for client meetings, business travel and coffee stockpiling expeditions. In all of these cases, access to the web can be invaluable. A plethora of mobile broadband hardware options abound – USB modems, built-in connectivity, express cards and many others. Any of these options will require a monthly service plan for access via the usual suspects (Verizon, AT&T, Sprint, etc.), but when WiFi hotspots aren't readily available or if you're simply on the go a lot, they can be a lifesaver. By far, my top recommendation for this type of device is a new introduction to the mobile broadband product family: MiFi cards.

MiFi Card

These credit card–sized devices are basically mobile wireless routers that create a personal WiFi bubble of several feet around the card. Not only is this incredibly cool, it's more useful than other mobile broadband products for a few reasons. Unlike laptop-specific cards and modems, a MiFi card is designed to connect a bunch of devices with no configuration at all. You don't have to think about the technology; it just works. Your laptop, smartphone and camera can all use this personal, portable WiFi network. You can even let amiable travel companions and colleagues in on your password-protected network, should you so choose. As a bonus, MiFi cards are a lot more durable than the rest of the hardware in this space. Salient USB dongles and express cards have a way of getting trashed by errant elbows and in-flight service carts. With a MiFi card, just switch it on and toss it back into a pocket or bag for safekeeping.

It is also important to note that many 4G-capable phones are offering hotspot service for a few extra dollars per month. It is an excellent option if you can plug your phone into a charging station while using it. Otherwise, battery life becomes a huge issue.

Create, Work, Do

Many of a SoHo's daily doings are covered in the preceding chapters. For the vast majority, basic office applications coupled with audio, video and image manipulation get the job done. However, really making a serious go at a true SoHo involves more than knowing a few tricks in Excel. You'll need to create an entire corporate ecosystem, often without the usual mechanisms of support: administrative, human resources, communications and information technology.

Instead, it's just you.

Don't fret! Sure, sizeable scale will still require new staff and procedures, but operating a seamless SoHo has never been easier than it is today.

Portable Document Files (PDFs)

For starters, pick up a copy of Adobe Acrobat. At its core, this is the software that allows creation of PDF files. While it has a few other bells and whistles – form creation, permissions, protections and collaboration tools – what really matters is becoming a power user with PDFs. With Acrobat, document designs can achieve a look, feel and function simply not possible with more basic document distribution software. Certainly, the ability to include video, customize every visual element and create interactive features in your document is a terrific reason to skill up on Acrobat, but it's not the best one. The number one reason to master PDFs is simple: PDF files look the same on every computer. No matter how much time you spend tweaking every last page break, boldface and column width on that critical Microsoft Word dossier and Excel report, once they're sent off, you lose control. Maybe the recipient has a different version of Microsoft Office, wreaking havoc on your carefully laid out work. Or maybe he's on a Mac and you're on a PC – an almost guaranteed formatting upheaval. For any number of reasons, documents that look great on one computer can look like garbage on another, unless the document is in PDF format. Become a master of the PDF file, or leave your digital impression to fate.

As a bonus, PDFs are often accepted as secure documents. Many businesses are now parsing through red tape electronically, forgoing the cumbersome FedEx and fax debacle surrounding physical paperwork. For contracts and agreements, simply scan your signature and email it back. There is also a formal method of creating a legally binding electronic signature in Adobe Acrobat.

For extra points, try scanning a version of your signature and use your new photo editing skills to affix it to other official communiqués like newsletters, memorandums and invoices.

Using a Scanner and PDF Files to Replace Your Fax Machine

Of course, just because you've chosen to live digitally doesn't mean the rest of the world has. For those luddites who won't accept digital transmissions, use a service like Send2Fax.com to send and receive faxes online. Be careful with choosing your online fax vendor: you want to choose a service that turns PDF files into faxes and vice versa. This way, you can send a PDF file as a fax by simply emailing it to the service. And when you receive an incoming fax via email from the fax service, it will already be in PDF format.

Accounting and Bookkeeping Software

No matter the size of your SoHo, at some point you're going to need help tracking finances. Keeping on top of receivables, payables, cash flow and the longer-view profit and loss situation is an arduous but essential task. Once again, plenty of software choices avail themselves to manage this front, but the best choice easily comes from long-standing industry leader Intuit, maker of Quicken and QuickBooks. Both pieces of software help manage personal and small business finances. While Quicken is easier to use, it's a more basic program that hides complex (but important) accounting functions and options for the sake of lessening the learning curve. Any small business responsible for payroll, invoicing and contracting or with plans to do so should opt for QuickBooks instead. Even a serious self-employed venture will quickly outgrow Quicken for lack of important fiscal analysis tools. As such, I strongly recommend that anyone who needs to compile financial documents of any kind opt for QuickBooks.

Additionally, I suggest checking out Mint.com. An online personal finance management tool, Mint allows you to sync your bank, credit, debt, real estate and investment accounts to a single in-the-cloud Mint profile. Mint is one of the most useful, intelligent startups of the Web 2.0 era. Transactions and transfers are automatically tallied and filed under specified and customizable accounts (e.g., rent, utilities and entertainment). Mint has a robust budget management tool that can create limits on these accounts, warning you when one goes over. The finances-at-a-glance utility of Mint is absolutely fantastic, too. As online solutions go, Mint is a nice way to keep an eye on your finances.

Meetings

For those pitches and presentations that deserve more than a phone call but less than a face-to-face encounter, I highly recommend GoToMeeting (www.gotomeeting.com). The conference call of the future, GoToMeeting is an online tool that allows you to host a meeting in which all attendees can speak to one another using their computer microphone, telephone and/or text chat. You can "share" your screen with other attendees, so they see what you see, work collaboratively on documents, switch presenters on the fly and even record the meeting for future reference. This is a terrific way to guide potential clients through a pitch or maintain cohesion when meeting with team members scattered around the globe.

Oh, and for those critical meetings that require being in the room, a word of advice: get a GPS device. The time saved, stress reduced and status gained from never being lost and late again are invaluable. If you're an Android user, Google's Navigation app is probably already loaded on your device. It is an awesome GPS app!

Phone

Cell phones are wonderful, but sometimes, like when they are out of batteries, out of signal or out of pocket, you just want a landline. A functioning SoHo needs a reliable landline connection with a modern, two-line business phone attached. Which service provider you choose is up to you, although it may be worth investigating Voice Over Internet Protocol (VOIP) as an option. These services use your broadband Internet connection, rather than traditional telephone connections, to make telephone calls. VOIP is usually cheaper than POTS (Plain Old Telephone Service), but occasionally runs into quality-of-service issues, notably a droning or popping characteristic in the sound of your voice. Generally, these issues are minor and infrequent, but something to consider when choosing your phone connection.

Regardless of which service provider you choose, consider Google Voice (www.google.com/voice). As with most things Google, Voice is not just incredibly cool, but exceedingly useful. Its "one number" feature allows you to create a brand new telephone number that rings all your phone lines (cell, work, home, etc.) when dialed. Alternatively, you can set your Google Voice number to ring certain phones when certain contacts call or during certain times of day. Obviously, this is a great way to ensure you don't miss a call when moving from location to location, but it's also a great way to let your contacts use the same phone number forever, even if you change service providers and receive a new phone number. My personal favorite feature is voicemail transcription, which automatically turns voicemail messages into text and delivers the message to you as an email. This is wildly useful, not just for checking messages in noisy environments, but because many people find email and text more manageable forms of communication; you can mark them for follow-up or search your email for the communiqué later. These are just two of the features of Google Voice. Others, like SMS to email, sharing voicemail, block/screen callers and personalized voicemail greeting, make it a no-brainer pick up for any SoHo worker. Oh, and yes, it's free.

Project Management

As more work comes in and your team expands, you may find the simple logistics of keeping projects on track an increasingly difficult task. There are many, many project management tools and services available for this type of coordination, but, as you may have come to expect, I prefer a simple, inexpensive and in-the-cloud solution to most others. Basecamp (www.basecamphq.com) is a good choice. A well-written piece of software, Basecamp is used by millions of users, from start-up entrepreneurs to the Fortune 500. It allows members of your team to communicate with each other in threaded forum/comment-style discussions, a great way to keep everyone in the loop and store conversations for reference later. Everyone can store and share key assets and files on a project-specific and company-wide basis. Managers can assign due dates, responsibilities and milestone markers, ensuring that projects stay on track and deliver on time. Best of all, the software integrates into your current email system, meaning many of these tasks can be accomplished directly through your current email client while remaining stored in an interactive online environment. That said, Basecamp is not for everyone. Because it is a cloud-based solution, when you're not online … you're out of touch.

Outsourcing

If things start getting serious, you may find yourself in need of some support. Those supplemental daily tasks – scheduling, customer service, data entry, and others – tend to get in the way of doing actual work. Consider hiring a virtual labor force to help out. For example, a virtual assistant who screens calls, schedules appointments and replies to basic correspondence is an inexpensive way to dramatically alter the professionalism your SoHo exhibits. Workers of this sort can be found through many services on the web; however, oDesk (www.oDesk.com) has emerged as an especially popular and effective virtual labor pool. On oDesk, freelancers and employers find each other through explicit job and hiring opportunities, choosing each other by reviewing ratings and feedback from previous engagements. The success and popularity of this service have been astounding. Job prospects have become quite broad, ranging from personal and administrative assistance to order processing and customer service to web design and copywriting. For an expanding SoHo, oDesk offers an inexpensive, self-contained way to scale effectively. For other recommendations on online tools to manage the offline world, visit www.OvercomingTheDigitalDivide.com.

Press and Promotion

If things start going *really* well, you're going to want to spread the good word.

While you may feel that seeking and managing press may be overkill for you and your small business, don't dismiss it out of hand. Some personal professional accomplishments – releasing a self-published work, incorporating an LLC, forming a major blog partnership – are worth trumpeting. Stodgy as it may seem, a well-crafted press release can yield real rewards for a growing small business. Send your press releases directly to local and trade publications, as appropriate. It's possible the story may be picked up by a news organization, furthering visibility dramatically. If you really want journalists to cover your story, you are going to have to contact them and pitch it. If you don't have the time or the contacts, there are many free online services, like PRlog.com and ClickPress.com, that will automatically distribute and publish your press release to a number of different sites, including news aggregators, such as Google News. For a modest premium, other services, such as Marketwire.com and PRnewswire.com, offer broader distribution and consultative services.

So what's the point of getting a press release published on the web wire, especially if nobody runs the story in a more mainstream outlet? Links. By tactically linking a press release back to your relevant website, you immediately generate dozens of inbound links from respected sources. While it is no replacement for genuine word-of-mouth endorsement from unique sources, this is a great strategy to get some promotional ground cover out there and force Google to pay a little more attention to you.

One Last Time

Finally, I'll end with an important reiteration: back everything up all the time! All these brilliant PDFs, illuminating financials and promotional releases can disappear in a flash. I mentioned briefly in the previous chapter how cheap and easy it is to back up data, but it really can't be stressed enough. Put a recurring weekly event in your calendar to transfer critical documents, files and data to an external hard drive or online storage space. Then do it religiously. Then find a redundant backup option, store it in a different physical location from your primary drive and back up your backup monthly. This sounds like overkill. It is not. Terrible, terrible things will happen to you if you don't heed these words. I'm not trying to be dramatic. The more digital you get, the more disastrous a hard drive crash, virus infection, office fire or mischievous ten-year-old nephew will be. For whatever reason, this tends to be the digital medicine nobody takes.

> *Three important things to remember: Back up important files daily. Back up important files daily. Back up important files daily.*

It's the good idea everyone perpetually plans to do next week. Don't wait. Do it now and make it routine. You'll thank me later.

Sync

With all these files flying back and forth among so many different computers and smartphones, it can be extremely difficult to keep version control or simply have the right file on the right device at the right time. The more people added to the equation, the exponentially more true this becomes. What you're really looking to do is synchronize your digital life, and the more digital your life becomes, the more pressing your need to sync it up. Generally, this means having any digitally stored information and data available to you or your colleagues on any given computing device all the time. This is why I have recommended cloud computing solutions so readily throughout this book. Delicious, Highrise, Gmail, Facebook and Google Reader are all fantastic examples of digital life in the cloud. If it's not already apparent, the magic of these services is that they are served online on demand, regardless of who is using them or what device they are being accessed on. This, in essence, is the simplest way to sync up every aspect of your digital life.

If this doesn't immediately appeal to you, just wait. It will. Ever miss an appointment because the entry made in your Outlook calendar at work wasn't available at home? Ever realize while you are traveling that your laptop doesn't have the phone number of a certain critical contact? Ever wish you didn't constantly have to email or load that one file you're working with onto a USB? All of these have very simple solutions in cloud computing. Need more convincing to move your workaday doings into the cloud? Steve Ballmer, CEO of Microsoft, has often said, "We're betting the company on the cloud." The company best known

> *Data you store in the cloud need to be backed up too!*

– and most financially fueled – by proprietary, locally based software has totally embraced cloud-based solutions. Follow its lead. Just remember: cloud-based data need to be backed up every day too!

Google Apps

Thankfully, it's really quite easy to get your SoHo running in the cloud. Your greatest ally in this is Google, hands down. The company's core technology (search), business model (ads) and umbrella offerings (apps) are entirely online.

It's Google's whole philosophy. While many of Google's applications are fantastic examples of in-the-cloud programs, the most common and critical are Gmail and Google Calendar. These two applications solve a huge swath of most of SoHo's syncing problems. Gmail is one of the most widely accessible, user-friendly and feature-rich email systems available anywhere. It can integrate directly into the mail application of almost any modern smartphone, and obviously, it keeps all of your email in the cloud and fully searchable, forever. In its premier edition (which costs only a few dollars per month), Gmail can take over as your unique domain's email server, among other business-oriented benefits. This means you get all the functionality of Gmail but can keep a custom @yourdomain.com address rather than the @gmail.com address.

Google Calendar is even better. Much like Gmail, Google Calendar can manage scheduling and appointment setting in an online interface, accessible from any web-connected device. It two-way syncs with Microsoft Outlook's calendar and Apple's iCal, meaning a change on Google Calendar is reflected in your Outlook calendar and vice versa. An iPhone's calendar application can directly integrate and sync with Google Calendar, a BlackBerry can be similarly synced by downloading the Google Mobile app and all Android smart devices are endemically Google compatible.

Think about those last two sentences for a moment.

Google Calendar integrates your desktop calendar, phone calendar and online calendar seamlessly; a change on any of them is reflected on all of them. This is *insanely* awesome. It used to be an expensive, complicated luxury, when it was even possible. And you can do it on your own, easily, for free.

As if this weren't enough, Google Calendar also allows multiple parties to see, share and manage individual calendars. In other words, you can create a personal calendar that only you can edit, allowing others only to see its scheduled appointments as "busy" or "free." You can then create a professional calendar which you and your assistant can edit but which allows everyone to see exactly what you are doing and when. Then you can create a calendar editable and viewable by everyone in your SoHo called "Conference Room," in which time in the SoHo's public meeting space can be reserved. This stuff used to be constant, convoluted logistical spaghetti. Now, easy as Google pie. Of course, Gmail and Google Calendar are only the two most common Google apps. Plenty of other applications, such as the project management tool Google Sites, offer incredibly inexpensive, intuitive ways to manage and scale a growing SoHo.

Dropbox

If Google solves most of a SoHo's syncing problems, Dropbox.com solves many of the rest. Dropbox is quite possibly the best online backup, file-sharing and syncing solution anywhere on the web. This incredibly intuitive system is loaded with features and offers up to 2 GB of storing and syncing free of charge, and up to 100 GB for paying customers. The service has both an online interface and a fantastic local tool that can be installed on any Mac, PC or Linux machine for simple drag-and-drop functionality. Any file uploaded to a Dropbox account is stored on its secure server and available through your online account on any web-connected device. This is an incredible way to keep key files a click away at all times. Additionally, you can set up shared folders that multiple parties have access to – a great place to keep documents everyone in your SoHo needs access to. Even better, you can use Dropbox as an FTP replacement. Instead of jumping through hosting hoops to transfer files too large for email, just upload the file to Dropbox's public folder, copy the web link and send it to your colleague, who uses the link to download the file directly from Dropbox's server. These problems – online backup, file sharing, FTP replacement – are rarely packaged in one service, let alone one as simple, elegant and *free* as Dropbox. For other resources on how to sync and manage online files, visit www.OvercomingTheDigitalDivide.com.

DIGITAL DICTIONARY

FTP (file transfer protocol):

The methodology that allows for the exchange and manipulation of files over the Internet. In practice, this is often used to transfer large files from one computer to another.

Chapter 10: Digital Domain

If you've come this far, you've acquired an impressive digital toolbox. You know the software. You've picked up the skills. You grok the culture. It's time to showcase it. Everyone should own and operate a digital domain, a little corner of the web to call your own. This is home base for your personal brand, the nexus of your network. It's a way for Google to find you, a place to direct attention and a chance to put your newfound powers to work.

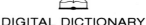

DIGITAL DICTIONARY

Grok (rhymes with "rock"):

A colloquialism favored by the digitally literate, engineers and geeks in general. Refers to a deep, integral understanding of something; an intuitive rather than instrumental grasp of a concept or culture gained through empathy and identity rather than memorization or abstract conceptualization.

Getting Started

First things first: you'll need to register a domain name, the identifiable bit of your web address. This can be as simple as your first and last name – the perfect choice if you want your website highly ranked on a Google search for your name. Of course, if your goals are a bit different – a digital space for your small business, an in-vertical resource or a community-specific blog – you may want to get a bit more creative with the name. In any case, you'll need to find out if that domain name is available. Many registration sites like 1and1.com and GoDaddy.com offer a straightforward, inexpensive registration service for your own domain name. Find an available, easy-to-convey domain name and purchase the domain registration.

Generally, .com is the preferable top-level domain option, as it's the most common and the default extension most people will use when entering a web address. Purchase additional domain extensions (e.g., .net, .biz, .org) if you want to ensure nobody poaches on your territory. Each domain shouldn't cost more than a few dollars per year. This process only reserves the domain address for you – staking a claim, so to speak. For a website to actually function, you'll also need to build a website and put it online. The geekspeak for this function is "host." You or a third-party service will host your website. The hosting service makes your website available to your users. If you're reading this book, there is a very small chance that you are going to host your own website. You will want to use a professional hosting service. Fees vary, based on usage, but generally, the more people who visit or "use" your website, the more expensive your hosting bill will be. This is an excellent problem to have. Almost any registration service will also offer hosting services, and it is often easier to register and host a website with the same service. For an up-to-date list of professional domain name registrars and recommended hosting services, visit www.OvercomingTheDigitalDivide.com.

Your Online Presence – Web or Blog

Before moving to the next step, it's critical to decide how, specifically, you want to appear to the online world. Generally, this decision breaks down to the choice between a website and a blog. It's not a mutually exclusive relationship (all blogs are websites), but rather a functionality decision. A website is a relatively static thing. It's a great place to put up your portfolio of work, sell services, house your bio and offer contact information. It's not the place for your résumé (use LinkedIn for that), but rather a fixed place for people to learn more about you. Every change requires going into the back end of the website and manually adjusting its HTML.

A blog, on the other hand – which may also contain sections for your portfolio, services, bio and contact – is a more dynamic web presence.

Will you regularly update your domain with commentary, links, articles, videos, photos and other media? Then you want a blog. Rather than a manually adjusting HTML, a blog has an online content management system (CMS), which is usually a simple WYSIWYG (what you see is what you get) interface allowing you to publish new content through your web browser. Blogs are a fantastic, arguably preferable, personal branding tool. Because they're updated so frequently and often linked to from outside sources, it's very easy for Google to find them. They can foster conversation and attract outside attention, helping you create a wider online network. The only trick is commitment and consistency. There is nothing more useless than a blog that posts only a handful of times a quarter, and nothing sadder than an abandoned blog that hasn't seen an update in months. If you can't commit to posting at least once (ideally a few times) each week and keeping pace, then don't start a blog. It'll just make you look unreliable.

Build It

Once you've secured a domain, purchased a hosting service and decided on what you want to accomplish, it's time to start building. This process can be as complex or as simple as you want it to be. The gamut of options is exhausting, but I feel comfortable recommending that you use one of the following four methods to build a website or blog: templates, Squarespace, WordPress or Outsource. Each has its own benefits and drawbacks, which I'll highlight briefly – it's up to you to decide which method best suits your needs.

Templates

If you plan to create a static website with the sole purpose of conveying information through text and media, an existing template may be the best option for you. Most registration and hosting services have simple, prebuilt websites you can choose from. By simply modifying the existing design and content within these templates, almost anyone can quickly and easily get a functional website up and running with minimal effort. Both GoDaddy.com and 1and1.com have "website builder" services available as part of their hosting bundle. While these templates are not ideal for a blog and won't offer much advanced functionality, they're perfectly suitable to create a basic, straightforward website.

Squarespace

For a bit more customization and complexity, Squarespace.com could be the way to go. Squarespace is a web-based environment for creating and managing websites of surprising complexity with tools of impressive simplicity. Featuring a drag-and-drop WYSIWYG interface, Squarespace is a fantastic option for anyone looking for additional customization and more robust functionality on their website. Squarespace can add data entry forms, photo galleries, social media integration and other wonderful features to your website while also offering inexpensive hosting services starting at just a few dollars per month. Additionally, Squarespace has its own blog software, making it a suitable choice for those looking to maintain regular site updates.

If there is a downside to Squarespace, it's that its intuitiveness comes with limitations. At a certain point, the functionality of a Squarespace site maxes out. While other services offer incredibly powerful website plug-ins and robust third-party development communities, Squarespace keeps things simple in favor of flattening the learning curve. Additionally, some have expressed concerns with Squarespace's SEO. As it's not an exact science, I won't comment other than to say

DIGITAL DICTIONARY

Plug-in:

A small piece of software that can integrate into larger software to extend or otherwise improve its capabilities.

it's a safe bet that other web-building tools probably have better abilities to drive SEO. It's not that a Squarespace site will never rank well on Google; it just may not rank as well, as fast or as high as similar sites more dedicated to SEO. If your web presence is aiming to be highly competitive, this is a cost well worth considering.

WordPress

One of the other web-building tools and industry stalwarts is WordPress. WordPress is the gold standard of blogging software. Open source and free to use, it is the largest blogging tool in the world. Because of its popularity, it has attracted a huge pool of developers, constantly improving the core code while creating thousands of plug-ins, widgets and design themes. As such, the functionality of WordPress is incredibly broad. Many of the biggest blogs in the world use WordPress, including major brand blogs like Ford, the *Wall Street Journal*, Sony and CNN.

To clarify, there are two ways to access WordPress technology, WordPress.com and WordPress.org. WordPress.com is a much simpler, web-based version of WordPress. It has limited design and functionality customization, has no ability to install plug-ins and will not allow advertising of any kind. Additionally, your site will contain an unsightly promotional suffix (i.e., www.domain.wordpress.com) unless you pay a fee. WordPress.org, on the other hand, removes these limitations while remaining free to use. Of course, all this whizbang means a more complex workflow. On WordPress.org, you download the WordPress software and install it on your host server, a bit of a trick in itself. Furthermore, the full onus of upkeep rests on your shoulders: maintaining adequate hosting, stopping spam, installing version updates and keeping regular backups of your site. This method of using WordPress is managed using an FTP client, so you'll need to familiarize yourself with tools like FileZilla (Windows) or Transmit (Mac). Needless to say, it's a more tech-heavy process. That said, it's not so wildly complex that I'm advising against it. The benefits of this self-hosted version of WordPress are invaluable, and getting it up and running is a fantastic trial by fire to prove your digital chops.

Outsourcing

Of course, if you disagree, there's always the easy way out. Outsourcing, to be exact. Since building websites and blogs can be a bit complicated – and let's face it, a professional is going to have design and development tricks you don't – it may be a worthwhile expenditure to just hire somebody to do it on your behalf. When choosing someone to work with you, you should have a list of desired features ready to present, and you should ask the potential vendor for live examples of previous similar work. Make sure those sites look good and function well. It should go without saying that this is a process worth the due diligence you'd give any potential vendor: ask for recommendations, shop the project around and make sure there is clear agreement as to what constitutes successful project delivery. One last bit of advice: you don't know what you don't know. If you want the best results, consider hiring a consultant to help you scope out your project.

Promote It

So you've arrived. Your website is on the World Wide Web. It looks beautiful, it's filled with brilliance and it works like a dream. And nobody but you knows it exists. It's a spot almost every new website finds itself in. Without dedicated promotion, it's nearly impossible to gain attention on the web. In fact, most digital creators acknowledge that compared to attracting viewers, the creative and technological effort of making web content is a breeze. There are no guarantees in life, and digital life is no exception, but there are a few proven techniques that will help increase the external recognition your work receives.

Search

Most often, the highest-return-on-energy method of promoting your digital domain is through search. This work falls into two categories: search engine optimization (SEO) and search engine marketing (SEM).

SEO is quite frankly a required component of any web endeavor. For many sites, it's the number-one source of traffic and one of the few ways to attract new visitors who've had no previous association with your web property. I spoke briefly about SEO in Chapter 4, and I'll expand a bit on the topic here, but truthfully, SEO is a subject deserving a book of its own. To that end, if you *really* want a deep understanding of SEO, one of my favorites is *The Art of SEO*[15] by Eric Enge, Jessie Stricchiola, Rand Fishkin and Stephen Spencer. This whopping tome, weighing in at 555 pages, is an exhaustive, detailed, yet surprisingly approachable read. It's arguably the definitive reference material for the current state of SEO, useful to layman and veteran alike. For those looking for a more Cliff-noted version, I

---

[15]http://www.artofseobook.com/

suggest "The 15 Minute SEO Checklist."[16]   While some of the terminology and recommendations within it may require some extra Google work on your part, the list is a terrific, quick sanity check on the most important elements of SEO.

While I strongly encourage you to investigate resources like the ones listed above for specific SEO techniques and implementation advice, it's just as important to understand *why* these techniques work at a conceptual level.   For that, we need to take a look under Google's hood.   At their core, search engines work by scanning or "crawling" every webpage in existence and indexing those pages in a massive database.   Those indexed pages are then tossed into a complex and proprietary algorithm determining which results to display when a user enters a search query.   The workhorse of this "crawling" process is called a spider.   At any given time, an army of these spiders are out exploring and retracing the web.   Your opportunity to optimize search results is by helping Google with these activities. Make your site easy to crawl and maximize your site's positive variables via the search algorithm.   In Chapter 4 we briefly outlined two critical factors in this equation: keywords and links.   By and large, keywords are used to optimize the result of a site's encounter with the search algorithm, while links optimize both the crawling and algorithmic processes.   A third factor, metadata, has waned in importance of late (important reminder: best practices of SEO change constantly) but remains a critical factor in helping search engines crawl and compute your site.   In this case, "metadata" is referring to additional information within a site's HTML.   HTML metadata are called tags, or meta tags, and they perform a wide variety of tasks.   Key among those tasks is a meta tag's ability to speak Google's language.   Think of meta tags as spider-whisperers.   Spiders don't view the web the same way a human does.   They ignore a lot, like images, audio, video, flash animations and JavaScript.   Meta tags, however, attract a spider's attention and can be used to convey important information about your site that would otherwise be lost on an ambivalent spider as it hurriedly crawls your site.

For any website, there are three pieces of metadata you should pay attention to: title, description and keywords.   The title tag is visible text that displays in the menu bar of a web browser.   This should act like a tagline – describe your site in a few words.   Simply put, the description tag is text describing your website.   It is how supporting search engines will describe your site when it displays it in search results. Almost all search engines will restrict how much space they dedicate to site descriptions, so limit your text to fewer than 165 characters.   The keyword tag isn't visible to users, but is scanned by spiders as a way of gleaning a broad-stroke

---

[16]http://www.webconfs.com/15-minute-seo.php

idea of what your site is about. Choose words and phrases that are used often within your site along with search terms you feel should result in links to your site. Any website-building toolset, like WordPress or Squarespace, will have settings at the administrative level allowing you to input this type of metadata.

Again, it's important to read up and keep up on specific techniques leveraging this conceptualization of the search process, but, grossly simplified, SEO does come down to those three factors: keywords, linking and metadata.

Paid Search Engine Optimization

Ever get spammed with an email that says something like, "We guarantee that we will get your site to the top of the Google listings," or some such nonsense? We all have. If the organization offering you this service is using spam to promote itself, just ignore it. However, there are some very reputable organizations that specialize in best practice search engine optimization. It is both an art and a science, and it is well worth the time it will take you to learn about it. For a list of reputable companies that specialize in SEO, visit www. OvercomingTheDigitalDivide.com.

Search Engine Marketing

Search engine marketing (SEM) is such a specialized business that it is the subject of hundreds of books, thousands of sites and blogs and dozens of annual business conferences. Although SEO and SEM work hand-and-hand, they are different from each other in one simple way. You almost always pay for your SEM placements. The most common SEM practice is buying premium placement display on search engine result pages through services like Google AdWords. This is where Google makes most of its money. With AdWords, advertisers make bids on certain search keywords in an auction-style market. The winning advertiser agrees to pay a certain amount every time a user clicks on its sponsored search result display. There are many businesses that can take advantage of Google's highly targeted, pay-for-performance SEM business model. But there is a very good chance that your business is not one of them. Because Google sells AdWords in an auction, popular keywords, like "plumber" or "dentist," are too expensive to buy. The calculation is simple. It's called return on investment or return on advertising spend. You just create a metric called "cost per acquired customer," or if you sell a product, "cost per sale." You calculate the efficacy of your SEM budget by determining how much it cost you per paid click to actually close a sale. A full tutorial in SEM is outside the scope of this writing, but if you want some excellent recommendations for SEM reading materials, visit www.

OvercomingTheDigitalDivide.com.

Outreach

All the search tricks in the world are no substitute for good, old-fashioned self-promotion. Building an authentic connection with the wider web community is part and parcel of attracting any sort of digital attention. Participating in, commenting on and contributing to other blogs and sites relevant to your area of expertise and interest are job one when promoting your digital domain, especially within the blogging community. Don't just spam blogs with naïve "Nice site. Check out mine" comments. Rather, add genuinely to the conversation with your unique perspective and insights and do so consistently, becoming a regular voice within online communities you admire. Then, as you gain acceptance, offer links to your own site when it's relevant and furthers the conversation.

Try emailing the site administrators and editors of select communities with feedback and comments. Build a relationship with them just as you would in real life; take interest in their lives and work, find areas of common interest and offer your assistance where it could be useful. Over time, you may discover mutually beneficial partnerships that help promote your respective communities, such as guest blogging for each other, exchanging blogroll links or swapping email lists.

In a similar vein, respond enthusiastically to those who reach out to you. Set aside time every day to reply to the comments your own blog receives and answer email correspondence. Those who take time out of their day to engage with your site are valuable digital allies, so shower them with reciprocal attention. Some will become evangelists for you and emerge as your site's version of the 1% rule.

Finally, don't forget to update your points of contact with links to your digital domain. Social media profiles, business cards, email signatures, site registrations, externally published bios and other static contact panes are the perfect place to include your web address.

Retention

Don't fall into the trap of thinking site promotion is all about luring new audiences. Just as important, if not more so, is retaining the audience you've already found. A single pageview from a new visitor who never returns isn't nearly as valuable as a fan who returns to your site, day after day, week after week. Allocate your time accordingly.

One of the best ways to retain visitors is by encouraging users to subscribe to your content. If you're publishing a blog, place an RSS icon linking to your RSS feed prominently on every page. Even better, encourage users to subscribe over email and start promoting your blog or site through a newsletter program. Newsletter programs are incredibly easy to set up and run using inexpensive services such as MailChimp.com or Aweber.com. A database of email subscribers is often one of the most effective and valuable promotional assets you can build. Just respect your audience's time and inbox-load. As a rule of thumb, don't send newsletters more than once a week, and if you plan to barter or monetize your email list, be sure those intentions are clearly stated in a privacy policy users can read before handing over their email address.

It is also important to follow strict bulk email rules. Put a "one-click" unsubscribe link at the top and bottom of each email. Put a copyright notice, your name, your company name, address and telephone number at the bottom of every email. Make sure that you instantly unsubscribe anyone who wants to be unsubscribed. Make this process easy. A small, self-assembled audience that wants your information is way more valuable than a large audience that ignores, trashes or deletes your unwanted messages.

That said, building and messaging subscribers is a great way to remind people of your site, pulling them back to your digital domain, but regardless of how users find you, once they've arrived, your aim is to deliver value. Good site design and navigation structure are the foundation of an inviting user experience, and consequently longer, higher pageview visits. Think about other websites you enjoy spending time on. What makes them easy to use? What encourages you to click around? Identify the aesthetic and functionality choices you find particularly effective and mimic them on your own site. Consider adding features that encourage exploration. Affixing tags, or topical keywords, to each post is a blogging best practice and great service to your audience. Each tag links to a list of all the posts marked with that tag. Take it one step further and use tags to support great discovery plug-ins and widgets, such as the ability to suggest related articles at the end of each blog post or a "tag-cloud" widget displaying the most popular tags on your blog. Most blogging software prompts you to add tags to any new post you create – take the extra few minutes and list them out.

Just be careful not to confuse blog tags with blog categories. Categories are another way to topically organize your posts. Often listed on the right-hand navigation of a blog, each category links to a list of all the posts within said category. While categories seem a lot like tags, in practice they're very different. Categories should be limited in number, fixed in placement and topically broad. Choose a dozen or two, don't alter them often and choose wide-ranging themes or concepts over specific issues or subjects.

Tags, on the other hand, can be organically developed, ever-widening in number and granular in focus. For example, if this book were a blog, each chapter would be a category: multifaceted subjects with broad themes which we outlined before the writing began. Tags would be developed from recurring, narrow topics that kept popping up throughout the writing process, such as Apple, Smartphones and Cloud Computing.

Of course, sometimes people just need to be pointed in the right direction. Consider adding a "best of" section somewhere in the blog's permanent navigation area, highlighting your personal favorite posts, the most popular posts of all time and the most commented posts. Some blogs do well by creating blog series that build over time, like "30 Days to Building a Better Mousetrap," or a narrative strung together from post to post. Series like this are great at keeping readers coming back for more, and should they prove popular, they are content to highlight in special editorial sections of your site. Experiment and play with different editorial and promotional strategies. Maybe your users would enjoy a random post button that draws up a random blog post. Maybe they'd like to vote in a poll that chooses what topic you'll write about next. Or maybe they'd like an opportunity to join you for a regularly scheduled live chat. No two audiences are exactly alike – it's up to you to get a handle on your audience's appetite and serve up what they want.

Just keep in mind, no matter how well promoted your site may be, it won't make up for lackluster or inconsistent content. Respect your audience by setting aside time to regularly update your site with content you're proud of and dedicate separate, but no less consistent, time to promoting it. Then, keep at it. Many new bloggers and site owners become disillusioned when their digital domains remain mired in relative obscurity for the first few months. Don't give up. It can take 3–6 months for search engines and the wider web community to embrace a new presence, and it's often a slow, plodding exercise in incremental gain for some time after that. This race rewards the tortoise, not the hare.

Analyze It

I've recommended a lot of strategic, technological and promotional techniques in this chapter. For many of those techniques, I've encouraged you to "try and see," making tweaks to execution and reinvesting in success based on results. While provoking and responding to direct user feedback are important, they're not even close to enough for this type of data-heavy decision making. What you really need is constant, quantitative analysis.

Analytics

For that, there is Google Analytics. Google Analytics is an in-the-cloud tool for scrutinizing website traffic in its many permutations: where users are coming from, what they are looking at, how long they stay, where they leave, user demographics, user loyalty and much more. It can even set up customized conversion goals and metrics, such as "Do 10% of all visitors to my newsletter page sign up?" Best of all, it's totally free and incredibly easy to set up – just drop a bit of their code into your website HTML. Visit www.google.com/analytics for step-by-step instructions.

Once you install Google Analytics, I imagine you won't have any trouble checking your traffic stats. It's addictive, fun and, as with all things Google, available on any web-connected device. Slightly more difficult is knowing what stats to focus on. As mentioned, Google Analytics is a wealth of data, and it can be a bit overwhelming to the uninitiated. While every metric has a time and place, I recommend focusing on the following.

Pageviews

Pageviews represent the total number of times the pages on a website are visited. This is the standard, bread-and-butter metric for judging the total visibility of a website. More pageviews translate quite directly to more attention. This is a top-level metric with many variables at play determining how many pageviews a site or page receives. Strive to grow your total domain pageviews month over month.

Bounce Rate

A site's bounce rate refers to the percentage of visitors who visit a single page of a website, then leave the site without viewing another. It's difficult to benchmark this metric. For e-commerce sites, social networking sites and sites relying on landing pages as a primary point of entry, a high bounce rate is a major cause for concern. For news, entertainment or other informative sites, it's less so; users enter a site looking for sports scores or to read a single news article, then pop away when finished. In any case, bounce rate can effectively be used as a measure of how relevant and interesting a site is to its users. Generally, a bounce rate higher than 70% indicates a problem. Strive to keep your bounce rate as low as possible by making your site easy to explore and click around on while ensuring inbound users land on pages relevant to what they are looking for.

Traffic Sources

Of course, you won't know what users are looking for unless you know where they are coming from. By reviewing your top sources of traffic, you'll better understand where to focus your efforts. Is there a particular referring site that's dumping a lot of traffic your way? Form a partnership and ask how you can get more visibility with that site's audience. If a particular social network or marketing program is proving especially successful, put more effort into that channel. Are you getting a lot of direct traffic? That means people aren't clicking on any links to get to your site, but rather are manually entering your web address in their browser. They might have bookmarked your site or are checking it based on offline referrals such as print collateral and personal recommendations. In any case, find ways to encourage those users to subscribe to your content – they're at risk of being lost.

Of particular note here are search keywords. Google Analytics knows what search keywords are driving the most traffic to your site. This is an *incredibly* powerful piece of information. Optimize your content and titling to leverage the keywords driving the most traffic to your site.

Content

Just as important as where users are coming from is what they are looking at. By identifying the content getting the most traction, you'll know what type of content is resonating with your audience, so make more of it! If you're lucky, you may find one of your posts on the receiving end of traffic from a front page Reddit or particularly popular StumbleUpon share. Maximize those eyeballs! Edit the post to welcome those users specifically in a special byline ("Welcome Reddit Users!"), and encourage them to subscribe to or bookmark your site.

When viewing any specific piece of content, you can explore the path users made around that content by clicking on the Navigational Summary option. This is a beautiful presentation of where users were before they landed on that page and where they went after viewing it. This can become an overwhelming data set, but it is wildly interesting. Try to identify patterns and problems that can be leveraged to siphon and dam traffic to your advantage.

DIGITAL DICTIONARY

Cookie:

A locally stored data file a user downloads when visiting a website. Cookies are used for various purposes, the most popular of which are tracking and user behavior monitoring.

Other Data Sets

While no web metric system is 100% accurate, Google Analytics gets pretty good. This is because Google installs its tracking cookie on every single visitor to your website, reporting back to you exactly where your visitors go and what they do while visiting your site.

But what if you want to compare your site to other sites?

Unfortunately, Google Analytics does not work for web properties you don't control. Many "best guess" tools exist, however, to monitor traffic on external sites. Most use a version of Nielsen's traditional television rating system, in which a statistically significant sample of web users installs technology that tracks all of their web use, and then that sample is extrapolated to census data.

Obviously, this is fraught with challenges. The sample population may or may not truly match total, global web-surfing habits; smaller sites and sites serving a niche audience can be overlooked and certain technical limitations have yet to be overcome. So take the data with a grain of salt, emphasize ratio comparisons over raw numbers and use multiple sources whenever possible.

The major players in web-wide metric monitoring at this time are Nielsen, ComScore Alexa, Quantcast and Compete. Each of these will deliver varying results, and each has its own advantages and drawbacks. A brief review of their features follows, but bear in mind that this is a rapidly changing paradigm. Visit www.OvercomingTheDigitalDivide.com for the latest resources and advice on web metrics.

Alexa

One of the earliest companies to try to reference and organize the web, Alexa Internet was scooped up by Amazon in 1999 and is now best known for its operation of alexa.com, an online repository of information where users can look at a specific website's visibility in the wider World Wide Web, expressed as a percentage of all global web traffic. Alexa is one of the longest-standing companies to offer this kind of service and boasts one of the broadest sample bases.

Of course, on the web, many times, first mover advantage isn't nearly as valuable as best mover advantage. Over the years, Alexa's data have become increasingly dubious and its interface less intuitive, and many web professionals now prefer other metric analysis tools.

Quantcast

Quantcast.com is a newcomer to the web media measurement game. While it offers a similar service to Alexa, it maintains an important distinction. Through its direct verification service, publishers and website operators can voluntarily install Quantcast's tracking code, essentially giving Quantcast direct, Google Analytics–like access to traffic data. This provides a dramatically more accurate representation of participating websites and expands the measurable data to demographical information, such as age, gender and income bracket.

Bear in mind that many sites do not opt into this verification service, and Quantcast's smaller sample base means some results may be suspect, and smaller sites may simply not index at all.

Compete

Another web traffic analysis service, Compete.com arguably has the broadest source material for its metric and measurement computation. Like most analytic services, it keeps the specifics proprietary, but it is known to be a mix of direct information from Internet service providers, opt-in verification, application partners and individual web users. It has an extremely easy-to-use interface and specializes on site-to-site comparisons – a great method of matching your web property against that of competitors. As an added bonus, the site operates an extremely insightful blog that crunches all that web data into really useful web usage intelligence reports.

Nielsen

Yes, the ubiquitous television scoring system has its long, reaching hand in web measurement too, taking the form of the Nielsen NetRatings service. It offers an impressive array of services beyond basic traffic analysis, such as audience segmentation, marketing ROI analysis, strategic guidance and extensive online and offline commerce monitoring. Those at Nielsen have actually proven to be relatively progressive thinkers in this space. In 2007 they publicly endorsed an internal shift of key metric weight from raw pageviews to time spent on site, meaning that they felt the average amount of time spent on a site was more important than how many raw hits the site received. It was a move demonstrating prescient understanding; a small engaged audience can be considerably more valuable than a large disinterested one. At the time this wasn't a particularly mainstream digital opinion. It has since become so, and Nielsen continues to lead at the cutting edge of web measurement and analysis.

The downside of all this is that Nielsen does not offer its service for free. A hefty cost makes this tool unrealistic for non-enterprise-level accounts.

ComScore

One of the most visible and preferred online marketing research and digital measurement companies, ComScore, operates in a capacity similar to that of the Nielsen NetRatings service. Many custom and advanced programs and services serve some of the world's largest companies.

Again, a sizeable fee structure makes ComScore an unrealistic option for non-enterprise-level accounts.

In any event, it's probably best to use as many of these analytics tools as you can to glean a broad-stroke picture of usage patterns and traffic across the web.

Chapter 11: One Last Thought

I have always hated the word "technology." It seems like a word that geeks and self-described smart people use to overly complicate the world. It's a word that sits on the border between terms of art and plain English. I'd like to suggest that from here on out, you replace the word "technology" with the word "tool." All tools are technologies. The wheel, a hammer, a pencil, and even paper are all tools that help us live better.

To that end, this book is a tool. Its purpose is to help you do a better job of living and working in an increasingly digital world. But, like so many tools, it can help you only if you use it correctly. This book is a starting point, and the online resources are a dynamic, ongoing set of reference points. Correctly applied, this tool will help you solve problems that you used to have to ask someone else to solve for you.

Remember: technology is meaningless unless it changes the way you behave. More importantly, it is meaningless unless it changes the way others behave too. Do you need to know everything about the latest bright, new, shiny object? Of course not. But if you have stayed with me to this point, you should now have a sense of how to determine if a new tool is worthy of your attention.

One last thought: the digital divide that we have been trying to overcome in these pages exists only in your mind. It isn't really a divide at all. To cross over safely and prosper, just keep an open mind and inject yourself in the process of doing digital life. Everything else will take care of itself.

Glossary

API (application programming interface): The part of a software program that allows the program to interact with other software. On the web, APIs are commonly made publicly available by proprietary developers in the hope of enabling and inspiring third-party development of supplemental software.

B-Roll: In the early days of filmmaking, the A-Roll was the roll of film with the primary action on it. The B-Roll was the roll of film with the insert shots and reaction shots on it, for example, interviewer head nods or product shots. Sometimes both A-Roll and B-Roll are shot with two different cameras (A & B), and other times all the shots are done with one camera and in no particular sequence. Today, B-Roll is slang for any shots you can use to move your story along or cover your mistakes. In practice, you can never shoot too much B-Roll.

Cloud computing: Internet-based computing, in which information, resources and software are supplied to the user online, rather than through installed programs.

CODEC: A portmanteau (a blending of two or more words) of "compressor-decompressor" or, more commonly, "coder-decoder." In practice, a CODEC allows your computer to record or play back audio, video or still computer files. Popular CODECs include H.264, AAC and MPEG.

Cookie: A locally stored data file a user downloads when visiting a website. Cookies are used for various purposes, the most popular of which are tracking and user behavior monitoring.

Creative Commons (CC): A nonprofit organization that manages various copyright licenses that communicate the rights a content creator wishes to reserve, waive or alter.

"The Daily Me": A term describing the daily consumption of news personalized toward individual taste, often through automated and algorithmic means. The term originated from Nicholas Negroponte, founder of the MIT Media Lab.

Digerati: A play on the word *glitterati* (*glitter* + *literati*) which used to describe the digital elite but has become synonymous with the less-laudable title of "geek."

Digital Immigrant: Refers to anyone who grew up without 21st- century technology (i.e., anyone born before 1970) but has adapted to and adopted its use to some extent. Digital immigrants often pick up the traits and characteristics of digital natives, such as a trial-and-error approach to technology and an appreciation of information filtering and processing over information retention.

Digital Native: Refers to anyone who grew up with 21st- century technology (i.e., anyone born after 1980). Digital natives share a common global culture that is defined by certain attributes and experiences related to how they interact with information technologies, information itself, one another and other people and institutions.

Domain: The part of website URLs you recognize. Domains are broken into two parts, the hostname and the top-level domain. The hostname is the unique bit - the google in google.com and the wikipedia in wikipedia.org. The top-level domain is the suffix after the hostname. Examples of top-level domains include .com, .org, .info and .edu. Top-level domains generally refer to online verticals and offer a cursory understanding of a website's purpose. The .com sites are for commercial purposes, .org sites are for nonprofit organizations, .info is for information-based websites and .edu indicates official educational facilities. Most top-level domains are not strictly regulated (though some, like .gov and .edu, are) but can generally be used as an accurate representation of a site's content.

Egosurf: A colloquialism for performing and investigating a Google search on one's own name.

FTP (file transfer protocol): The methodology that allows for the exchange and manipulation of files over the Internet. In practice, this is often used to transfer large files from one computer to another.

Geotag: To add geographically relevant data to various forms of media. In practice, this often results in latitudinal and longitudinal coordinates being stored within everything from photographs to Twitter updates.

Grok (rhymes with "rock"): A colloquialism favored by the digitally literate, engineers and geeks in general. Refers to a deep, integral understanding of something; an intuitive rather than instrumental grasp of a concept or culture gained through empathy and identity rather than memorization or abstract conceptualization.

IP address (Internet protocol address): The numerical label assigned to all digital devices using the Internet. The most commonly used format is a set of four numbers separated by three periods (e.g., 192.168.1.1).

MAC address (media access control address): A unique, alphanumeric code used to identify a piece of Internet-connected hardware.

Metadata: Data that describe other data. More generally, metadata are additional information stored within various forms of media and electronic files such as photographs, videos, documents, websites and database entries. Metadata encompass all kinds of information like keywords, date/time stamping, author identity and geographic info.

Micro-celebrity: The web-centric phenomenon of being extremely well known to a group of people. The number of followers can be very small (e.g., the foodie within a circle of friends) to relatively large (e.g., A-list bloggers, Internet executives and web-show stars).

Open source: Generally, refers to software whose source code is publicly available. Open source software permits its users to study, modify and improve upon it, often resulting in collaborative, group-developed software. WordPress and Linux are extremely popular examples of open source software.

OS (operating system): A piece of software that provides the user interface environment in which other software runs. The most famous example of an OS is Windows, but all modern pieces of computing hardware have some form of OS running on them.

Plug-in: A small piece of software that can integrate into larger software to extend or otherwise improve its capabilities.

Quad-split, first-person shooter: "Quad-split" means splitting a video screen into four quadrants. "First-person shooter" is the generic term for bang-em-up, shoot-em-up video games where gameplay is predominantly from the protagonist's point of view.

RSS (really simple syndication): A tool used by online publications that groups all their articles into one easy-to-read "feed," or chronological list. Avid online readers use RSS to group all of their favorite online publishers in one place, which can be consumed in many different ways, including on their Google homepage, in Microsoft Outlook and on a smartphone. Online readers tend to consume from a large selection of varied sources, which if read in full would be haltingly cumbersome. RSS features an easy-to-skim "title and heading"-style display, allowing readers to pick and choose which articles they want to skip and which to spend time with.

Web 2.0: Often used to describe the perception of a generational shift in web development and web design. However, it was actually the name of an O'Reilly trade conference that occurred when the shift from rich data websites to rich media websites began.

CPSIA information can be obtained at www.ICGtesting.com
Printed in the USA
LVOW031921141211

259421LV00014B/79/P